BETTER HOMES AND GARDENS®

COUNTDOWN *to* CHRISTMAS

CHRISTMAS 'ROUND THE CORNER

BETTER HOMES AND GARDENS ®

Countdown to Christmas

CHRISTMAS 'ROUND THE CORNER

CRAFTS EDITED BY KARIN STROM

RECIPES BY KATHY BLAKE

Better Homes and Gardens ® Books

Des Moines, Iowa

Better Homes and Gardens®Books, an imprint of Meredith®Books:

President, Book Group: Joseph J. Ward
Vice President, Editorial Director: Elizabeth P. Rice
Executive Editor: Maryanne Bannon
Senior Editor: Carol Spier
Food Editor: Joyce Trollope
Associate Editor: Ruth Weadock

Countdown to Christmas: **CHRISTMAS 'ROUND THE CORNER**
was prepared and produced by
Michael Friedman Publishing Group, Inc.
15 West 26th Street
New York, New York 10010

Editor: Karla Olson
Production Editor: Loretta Mowat
Art Director: Jeff Batzli
Designer: Tanya Ross-Hughes
Photography Director: Christopher C. Bain
Illustrations: Roberta Frauwirth
Crafts Directions: Peggy Greig
Photography: Bill Milne

ISBN: 0-696-00048-2
Library of Congress Catalog Card Number: 93-080862

10 9 8 7 6 5 4 3 2 1

Printed and bound in China

Our seal assures you that every recipe in *Countdown to Christmas: CHRISTMAS 'ROUND THE CORNER* has been tested in the Better Homes and Gardens®Test Kitchen. This means that each recipe is practical and reliable, and meets our high standards of taste appeal. We guarantee your satisfaction with this book for as long as you own it.

All of us at Better Homes and Gardens®Books are dedicated to offering you, our customer, the best books we can create. We are particularly concerned that all of our instructions for making projects are clear and accurate. Please address your correspondence to Customer Service, Meredith®Press, 150 East 52nd Street, New York, NY 10022.

If you would like to order additional copies of any of our books, call 1-800-678-2803 or check with your local bookstore.

ACKNOWLEDGMENTS

Karin Strom would like to acknowledge the following people: Peggy Greig, Roberta Frauwirth, all the talented crafts people who contributed, Karla Olson for her perseverance, Carol Spier for her patience, Chris Bain for his moral support, The Millers of Glen Ridge, New Jersey, and Ellie Schneider of Hope, New Jersey, for use of their lovely homes during photography, and, of course, Colin, Viola, and Nadine for being there during a year of Christmas.

Kathy Blake would like to acknowledge the following people: Amelia Franklin, Gail Berry, and Laurie Middleton for help with testing and tasting, and Joyce Trollope and the Better Homes and Gardens® Test Kitchen for more testing and tasting.

Contents

INTRODUCTION

If you're someone who loves to create a personal Christmas each year, baking delectable treats for guests and crafting delightful gifts and decorations by hand, you know that Christmas can be a hectic climax of celebration and gift-giving. In **Better Homes and Gardens**® *Countdown to Christmas* series, you'll find a step-by-step guide to the easiest and most memorable holiday season ever.

Although the holiday is getting closer, there is still plenty of time to make this Christmas special. *Countdown to Christmas: Christmas 'Round the Corner* offers delicious recipes to freeze in anticipation of the holiday season, and charming, not-too-time-consuming gift ideas to craft ahead of time. Entrées, desserts, side dishes, and breads can be squirreled away in the freezer, then popped into the oven or microwave before serving. These lovely decorations include easy techniques such as fabric painting, appliquéing, woodworking, and jewelry-making.

It's not too late (or too early) to take advantage of the recipes and crafts projects in other *Countdown to Christmas* volumes. *Christmas On Its Way* is filled with fantastic storable recipes—jams, jellies, spice mixes, and more—and exquisite make-ahead gifts and accessories, each of heirloom quality, each a personal expression of appreciation and love. *'Tis the Season* is filled with quick, last-minute gifts and decorating projects for the time when you're busiest. In it you'll find recipes for fabulous feasts and holiday entertaining, with menu suggestions that can (but don't have to) incorporate many of the foods you prepared from the pages of *Christmas On Its Way* and *Christmas 'Round the Corner*.

Better Homes and Gardens® *Countdown to Christmas* series is full of delicious Christmas recipes and great gift and decorating ideas. Each volume includes timely recipes and complete directions for crafts, and can be enjoyed on its own. Together, the books will really help you plan your holiday ahead and stay on track. If you wish, you can follow the suggestions for using foods you've prepared earlier or scraps left from your heirloom projects, but—even if you didn't have a chance to freeze your pie filling when the fruit was fresh or make the Pine Tree Quilt—you'll be able to complete any of the recipes or projects you wish.

There's no time like Christmas, with its warm well-wishing and gifts of love, enchanting decorations, and mouthwatering cuisine. There's plenty of time before Christmas for planning ahead—to make the most of the season as it arrives, so you can share in its joy and celebrate in style.

CHRISTMAS CRAFTS

PART

★
1

Now

is the time

to begin a couple

of fairly ambitious projects,

whether Christmas decorations

or handmade gifts. Decide which gifts

you will make for whom and get started.

Think about what entertaining you want to

do and what you need to do around the house before

the holiday season. Here are numerous engaging ideas for

holiday decorations and enticing gifts. The projects use a variety

of techniques, from painting and decoupage to needlework and wood-

work. However, none are so complicated or time consuming that you can't

finish them before the holidays, if you plan carefully and make time to work on

them. From a lovely

holiday welcome mat to

scarves, ties, and storage

boxes, the projects will

add beauty and plea-

sure to your holidays.

CHAPTER 1

Home for the Holidays

SPREAD MORE CHRISTMAS CHEER
AROUND YOUR HOME THIS YEAR BY
ADDING A FEW HANDCRAFTED
TOUCHES. PAINT A CHARMING
WELCOME MAT TO GREET GUESTS.
CREATE A TRIO OF SOPHISTICATED
HOLIDAY POTS FOR YOUR CHRISTMAS
PLANTS. APPLIQUÉ HOUSE PLACE
MATS WILL GIVE YOUR TABLE A
COZY, FESTIVE FEEL, WHILE THE
SLEIGH FULL OF FLOWERS WILL
BRING EVERLASTING BEAUTY.

WELCOME MAT

Roll out a colorful painted rug to welcome holiday guests this Christmas season. With all the busy comings and goings the holidays bring, it's both fun and practical to have a new rug for your entryway or in front of the hearth.

Inspired by patchwork quilt patterns, this simple geometric design is easy to paint on to a woven jute rug and can be done as shown or adapted to fit the rug you find by increasing or decreasing the size of the outer border.

SIZE

- Rug is 31" x 48".

YOU WILL NEED

- 31" x 48" natural colored jute rug
- 2 oz squeeze bottles acrylic paint: 2 red, 3 blue, 2 green, 1 yellow, 1 gold, 1 wine
- Stencil paper and stencil brushes, 1/2" to 3/4" diameter
- Paper plate and masking tape
- Metal ruler, craft knife, and pencil
- Acrylic satin-finish sealer

DIRECTIONS

NOTE: Let paints dry completely between steps. When painting near masking tape, it is best to "stomp" brush in an up-and-down motion, as you would in stenciling, to achieve a crisp and clean square.

PREPARE STENCILS: Enlarge star pattern on page 18 (see above, "Enlarging Patterns"), and trace onto stencil paper. With craft knife, cut out star for template, keeping star stencil section clean of any cuts. Both star template and star stencil will be used as stencils.

ENLARGING PATTERNS

With ruler and pencil, extend the grid lines over the diagram. On paper, draw a grid of squares in the size indicated by the scale given with the diagram, being sure your grid has the same number of rows and columns of squares as the original. Refer to the diagram and mark the full-size grid where the pattern lines intersect with the grid lines. Connect the markings. Refine any details if necessary.

PAINTING: Measure and mark 3 1/4" in from each outside edge of rug. Lay masking tape along inside of each line to create a straight, sharp paint line; tape should overlap to expose a 3 1/4" square at each corner. Squeeze red paint directly into corner squares and, using stencil brush, paint surface of corner square. Lift and remove corner masking tape. When red paint is thoroughly dry, cover sides of corner squares with masking tape to protect from outer border paint. Paint all four outer borders, in same manner as squares, with green paint. Tape outer borders with masking tape to protect painted areas. Following photograph, position star stencil in each corner, butting star motif against outside borders. Tape down to secure. Mix 2 tablespoons yellow with 1 tablespoon gold in a paper plate to get desired color. Paint star with yellow/gold mixture. When dry, measure and mark 8" in from outer

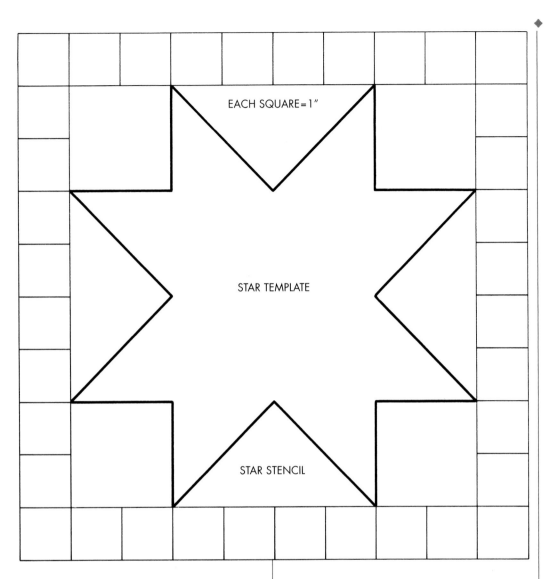

EACH SQUARE=1"

STAR TEMPLATE

STAR STENCIL

HOLIDAY POTS

Planted with topiaries or small evergreens, these unique designer pots will certainly be noticed by your guests this Christmas season. Because they are coated in polyurethane, they are suitable for a covered entryway, but shouldn't be exposed to harsh winter weather. By a door, flanking the fireplace, or as centerpieces on a table, these pots will add flair to your holiday decorations.

Make a pair of identical pots or mix and match as we've done here. Herb plants such as rosemary are a refreshing alternative to ordinary greens and are, in fact, used traditionally at Christmas in the Mediterranean countries.

SIZES

- Assorted clay flowerpots are 6", 7", and 8".

YOU WILL NEED

FOR ALL POTS:
- 6", 7", and 8" clay flowerpots
- 2 oz squeeze bottles acrylic paint in red, light blue, dark blue, and tan
- Gel medium or white glue/water mixture
- Water-based waterproofing sealer
- Paintbrushes

FOR FABRIC POT:
- ¼ yd fabric
- Synthetic gold leaf

FOR DECOUPAGE POT:
- Bay leaves
- Crackle paint
- Paper cutouts in desired motifs
- Hot-glue gun and glue sticks

borders on all sides for inner borders, using masking tape in same manner as for outer borders. This will make an 8" square around each painted star. Tape outer borders with masking tape to protect them, and paint inner borders with blue paint. Tape edges of each 8" star square to protect blue borders. Firmly hold star template on painted star to protect star and paint remaining square wine. Tape inner edges of blue border to protect them, and paint inner rectangle with yellow/gold mixture. Position star stencil so three stars will fit

- *Welcome Mat Star Template and Stencil*

evenly in rectangle, without touching. One at a time, paint stars red. Remove all masking tape and touch up any areas, if necessary. Spray with two coats of sealer.

FOR SPONGE POT:

- Kitchen sponge with scouring surface
- Stiff-bristle artist's paintbrush
- 2 oz squeeze bottle acrylic paint in gold

DIRECTIONS

NOTE: Let paints and sealers dry completely between steps. Mix equal parts of white glue and water to use in place of gel medium.

FOR ALL POTS: Following manufacturer's instructions, paint inside and outside of pot and saucer with waterproofing sealer.

FABRIC POT: Paint inside and outside of rim red. Paint rim with gel medium or glue/water mixture. Following manufacturer's instructions, gild rim with synthetic gold leaf. Cut a piece of fabric as wide as the height of the pot from bottom of rim to bottom plus ½", and as long as the circumference plus ½". Paint body of pot with gel medium or glue/water mixture. Wrap pot with fabric, placing top edge flush with bottom of rim and overlapping at sides. Smooth out any air bubbles with your fingers as you work. Fold lower edge under ½" to bottom of pot. Apply one coat of sealer.

DECOUPAGE POT: Paint body of pot red and rim light blue. Following manufacturer's instructions, paint body of pot with one coat of crackle paint. Paint body dark blue to reveal red underneath when paint crackles. Cover back of paper cutouts with gel medium or glue/water mixture and attach as desired, smoothing out any air bubbles with fingers as you work. Be sure to cover entire back of cutouts with gel medium and smooth edges to secure. Apply one coat of sealer. Using hot-glue gun and following photograph, attach bay leaves, overlapped, around pot rim.

SPONGE POT: Paint entire pot dark blue. Paint body of pot tan and, following photograph, paint sawtooth pattern on rim. Gently scrub pot with scrubber side of kitchen sponge to remove tan paint and allow blue to show through. Following photograph and using stiff-bristle artist's paintbrush and gold paint, highlight sawtooth pattern. Apply one coat of sealer.

SLEIGH FULL OF FLOWERS

Lush dried hydrangeas and vibrant freeze-dried roses fill the Fruitful Sleigh, a project from Better Homes and Gardens ® *Christmas On Its Way*. The rich colors of the flowers and faux fruits perfectly complement the mellow tones of the painted designs, but you can use any interesting container with complementary color and texture.

DRYING HYDRANGEAS

Autumn is the season for harvesting hydrangeas. The variety that dries the most successfully is the white or 'Pee Gee' hydrangeas, sometimes called "tree hydrangeas." The key to maintaining the perfect blooms is to let them "harden off" on the bush. The timing is tricky, as the blooms must be cut before a hard frost but after they have taken on a pinkish cast.

The best way to dry the flowers is to remove the leaves, tie the ends of several stems together with elastic or string, and hang them upside down in a dry spot, such as from the rafters in an attic.

Displayed on a side table in an entryway or used as a centerpiece, this striking floral arrangement will look spectacular for many seasons.

SIZE

- Sleigh is 14" long.

YOU WILL NEED

- Freeze-dried roses, cockscomb, and seed pods
- Air-dried hydrangeas
- Eucalyptus
- Artificial lady apples
- Artificial champagne grapes
- Sheet moss
- 1 block floral foam
- Masking tape
- Floral wire and picks

DIRECTIONS

Tape foam in sleigh. Cover entire block of foam with sheet moss. Following photograph, arrange and secure artificial fruit and dried flowers in foam as desired, using floral wire and picks as needed. Fill spaces with eucalyptus and roses.

APPLIQUÉ HOUSE PLACE MATS

These festive place mats make setting a holiday table so simple. Appliqué houses have welcoming wreaths on the doors, and the windows give a glimpse of the Christmas tree inside.

Make a pair for the center of a table or stitch a place mat and napkin set for each family member to enjoy all through the holiday season. This project is a great way to use any fabric scraps you have. Although a specific color key is given for one of the place mats, the other mat is completely different and shows that you can combine fabrics and colors however you like.

SIZE

- Each finished place mat is 12"x 17".

YOU WILL NEED

FOR EACH PLACE MAT AND NAPKIN:
- ¾ yd small print fabric in medium green for place mat front and back
- ½ yd each 3 small print fabrics in dark green, gold, and dark brown
- ¼ yd each 3 small print fabrics in off-white, medium red, and red
- Small amount green holly patterned Christmas fabric for tree and wreath
- Small scraps of bright red for bow
- 1 yd each fusible interfacing and paper-backed fusible web
- Matching thread
- Scissors, cardboard, and ruler

DIRECTIONS

NOTE: Refer to color key on page 25 for which fabrics to use for place mat pieces.

PLACE MAT: Enlarge pattern pieces at right (see page 16, "Enlarging Patterns"). From medium green, cut two full house pieces for front and backing. Following manufacturer's instructions, fuse interfacing to wrong side of front house piece. Fuse web to backs of appliqué fabrics. Following pattern and photograph, cut out appliqué pieces and assemble on front house piece. Fuse in place. Machine appliqué around each piece, using a narrow satin stitch and matching thread. Following pattern, with darker thread, work narrow satin stitch across D windows where indicated by dotted line. Press. With wrong sides together, pin appliquéd front piece to backing piece. Cut out two 1¼" wide bias strips, one 17" long and one 40" long, piecing if necessary. Fold each long edge ¼" to wrong side and press. Fold in half lengthwise, with wrong sides together, and press. Fold 17" bias strip over lower edge of place mat pin and top-stitch in place. Fold short ends of 40" piece ¼" to wrong side and press. Beginning at either lower corner and overlapping one end of 17" bias strip, fold 40" piece around the remaining outside edges of entire place mat, easing around corners, and slipstitch in place.

NAPKIN: Cut 16" square of E fabric. Serge or work close zigzag stitch over edges. Fold all edges ¼" to wrong side and topstitch in place.

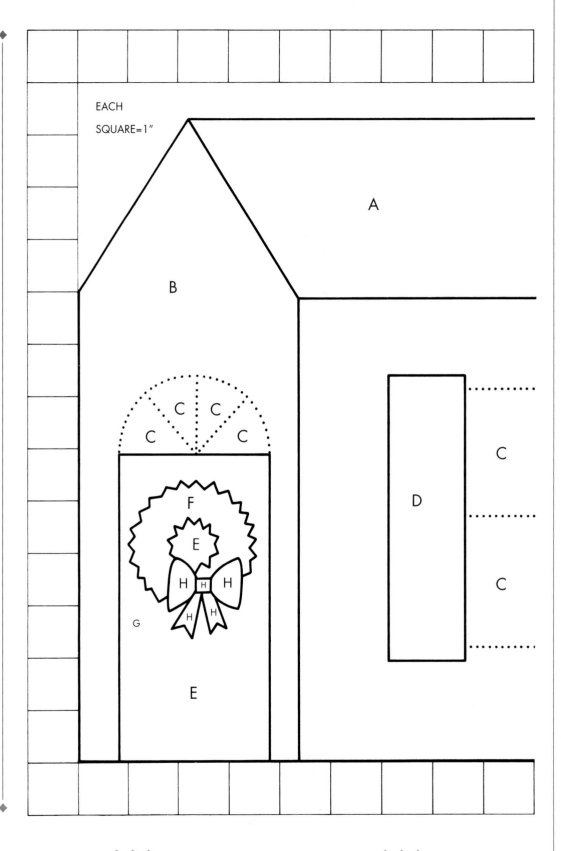

EACH SQUARE=1″

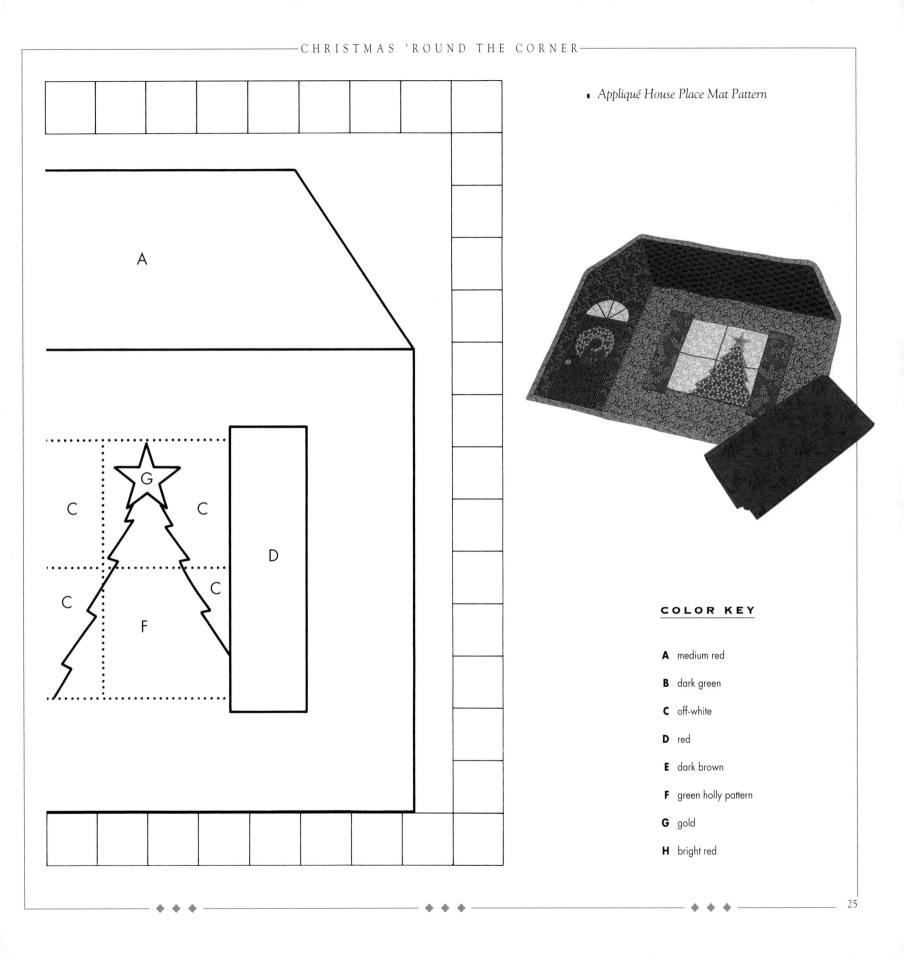

■ *Appliqué House Place Mat Pattern*

A

C

C

G

C

D

C

F

COLOR KEY

A medium red

B dark green

C off-white

D red

E dark brown

F green holly pattern

G gold

H bright red

Trimming the Tree

PULLING OUT THE FAMILIAR DECORATIONS HEIGHTENS THE ANTICIPATION FOR CHRISTMAS. THIS YEAR, UPDATE YOUR DECORATION COLLECTION BY CREATING HANDMADE ORNAMENTS, ADDING A FOLKSY FATHER CHRISTMAS TO YOUR FAMILY, OR FASHIONING GLORIOUS WOODEN ANGELS. GET THE KIDS INVOLVED IN MAKING THE FELT ADVENT CALENDAR. COUNTING THE DAYS UNTIL CHRISTMAS WILL TAKE ON A WHOLE NEW MEANING.

LACE ORNAMENTS

Delicate lacy ornaments are made with doilies and ribbons. An entire tree decorated with these lace shapes and wrapped in a red ribbon garland would be perfect in a Victorian parlor. Choose ribbon colors that coordinate with your own color scheme.

SIZE

- Ornaments are approximately 4".

YOU WILL NEED

FOR ALL FIVE ORNAMENTS:
- 1 bottle fabric stiffener
- 2 round cotton scallop-edged doilies, 7" diameter
- 1½ yds cotton lace, 2" wide
- 1 yd scallop-edged cotton lace, ¾" wide
- 1 spool each green satin ribbon, ⅛" wide, and red picot-edged ribbon, ³⁄₁₆" wide
- 1 package each small and medium red ribbon roses
- 3" diameter plastic foam ball
- Straight pins, plastic wrap, foam board or corrugated cardboard, and stiff tracing paper
- Sharp pointed scissors, plate or pie pan, newspaper, and cloth
- Hot-glue gun and glue sticks

DIRECTIONS

NOTE: Follow manufacturer's instructions for using fabric stiffener. It is easiest to saturate the lace in the stiffener in a plate or pie pan. Blot excess with a wet cloth before placing lace on templates.

TO MAKE A NOSEGAY: Glue three ribbon roses, using small or medium as specified, together from underside in a triangular pattern. Cut two strips of green satin ribbon, each 1¼" long. Overlap in a crisscross manner and glue to the back of ribbon roses. Add other ribbons as shown. Cut all ends of ribbons, streamers, and bows diagonally.

PREPARATION: Cover flat surface with newspapers. Enlarge patterns on page 30 (see page 16, "Enlarging Patterns"), and trace shapes onto stiff tracing paper to be used as templates. Place plastic wrap over templates and pin to foam board or cardboard. Refer to photograph to arrange trims.

SQUARE: Cut a 2" square from 2" wide lace. Saturate in fabric stiffener and place on plastic wrap over pattern template. Press flat. Cut four lengths of ¾" wide lace, each 3½" long, centering scallop motifs. Saturate and place two strips on opposite sides of square, making sure sides touch center square. Press flat. Trim ends of strips to miter. Repeat for remaining sides, folding ends under to miter corners. Pin in place. Allow to dry. Trim excess at corners with sharp scissors when piece is dry. Fold and glue a 6" piece of red ribbon on wrong side at one corner for hanging loop. Cut two pieces of red ribbon, each 12" long, and make two bows, each approximately 3½". Following photograph, arrange on top of each other and glue together. Cut two pieces of red ribbon, each 6" long, for streamers, and glue in place at back of bows. Cut two pieces of green ribbon, each 3" long, and glue in crisscross on top of bows. Make nosegay, using medium ribbon roses, and glue on top of green ribbon. Glue entire bow arrangement on right side in corner opposite hanging loop.

My friend Ellie and I exchange Christmas ornaments each year. It is a lovely way to renew the bonds of friendship, while adding to our collections of ornaments. Handmade ornaments make an especially thoughtful gift. If you are spending time in someone's home over the holidays, consider giving them a special ornament as a house gift.

FAN: Cut one round doily in half. Saturate half-doily in fabric stiffener and place on plastic wrap over pattern template. Evenly pinch small pleats at lower edge to form a fan shape. Pin outside edges flat. Fold raw ends under ¼" and press down. Allow to dry. Cut a 12" piece of red ribbon and tie into a 3½" bow. Cut two pieces of 6" red ribbon for streamers and glue to back of bow. Make nosegay, using medium ribbon roses, and glue together on top of bow. Glue nosegay, streamers, and bow in place on right side at bottom of fan. Fold and glue a 6" piece of red ribbon on wrong side at top of fan for hanging loop.

WREATH: Cut a 18" piece of 2" wide lace. Saturate in fabric stiffener and place on plastic wrap over pattern template. Evenly pinch pleats to gather center of circle, using lace motifs as a guide. Fold one raw end under and lap over remaining raw end of lace. Allow to dry. Make three nosegays, using small ribbon roses. Glue one nosegay over overlap of lace. Following photograph, glue remaining nosegays evenly spaced around wreath. Fold and glue a 6" piece of red ribbon on wrong side at top of wreath for hanging loop.

STAR: Using doily, cut out five scallop-edged motifs, each about 2½" long. Saturate in fabric stiffener and place on plastic wrap over pattern template. Evenly pinch centers of motifs to make pleats for center of star. Pin points of motifs to points of star template, pulling on doily to flatten. Overlap inside center of star and press together. Allow to dry. Fold and glue a 6" piece of red ribbon to wrong side of one point of star for hanging loop. Cut a 10" piece of red ribbon and tie into a 2½" bow. Glue one medium ribbon rose on two small pieces of 1" long green ribbon, arranged in crisscross manner. Glue to knot of bow and glue bow on right side at same place as hanging loop.

BALL: Cover foam ball with plastic wrap to use as a mold. Cut six 3½" pieces of 2" wide lace. Saturate one piece in fabric stiffener and wrap over foam ball. Smooth lace over ball, keeping it in a straight line. Pin edges of lace down, easing in any excess lace. Allow to dry; remove from ball. Repeat with remaining pieces. When all are dry, take three curved pieces and pin to ball, trimming ends of lace into points and fitting to ball with no overlaps. Glue these three pieces together, forming a hemisphere. Repeat with remaining three pieces. Remove from ball. Glue two hemispheres together and cover raw edge where joined with one long piece of ribbon. Fold and glue a 6" piece of red ribbon to top of ball for hanging loop. Cut three pieces of green ribbon, each 1½" long, and arrange in crisscross around hanging loop. Following photograph, glue four medium ribbon roses around hanging loop. Cut four pieces of red ribbon, each 4" long, and one piece of green ribbon, 2" long, for streamers. Using green ribbon folded in half, glue all streamers to bottom of ball. Cut three pieces of green ribbon, each 1½" long, and arrange in crisscross around streamers. Glue four medium ribbon roses around streamers.

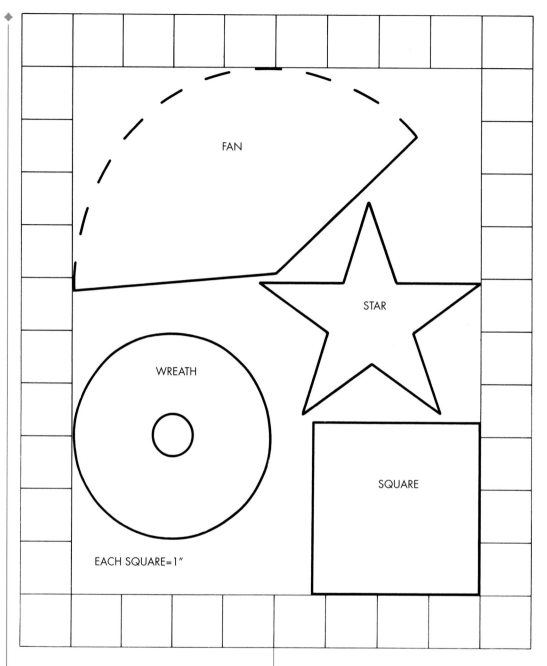

FAN

STAR

WREATH

SQUARE

EACH SQUARE=1"

▪ *Lace Ornament Patterns*

SAMPLER ORNAMENTS

Using motifs borrowed from the Home and Hearts Sampler from Better Homes and Gardens® *Christmas On Its Way*, these charming ornaments are cross-stitched, trimmed with lace, and stuffed. For a country or traditional setting, consider a tree decorated with Sampler Ornaments and festooned with a cranberry and popcorn garland.

SIZES

- Finished ornaments are 3" to 4".

YOU WILL NEED

FOR ALL SIX ORNAMENTS:

- ½ yd off-white 14-count Aida cloth
- ¼ yd red 14-count Aida cloth
- 1 skein each embroidery floss in light green, dark green, bright red, dark red, and off-white
- ½ yd green twisted cording, ½" diameter
- 1 yd off-white lace, ½" wide
- ½ yd red ribbon, ⅞" wide
- Embroidery hoop and needle
- Sharp scissors and masking tape
- Polyester stuffing

DIRECTIONS

FOR ALL ORNAMENTS: Tape edges of cloth to prevent raveling. Do not cut out ornaments until all cross-stitching is complete. With contrasting thread, baste horizontal and vertical centers of fabric. Center design on fabric, matching fabric center with center of chart. Following chart and key, work cross-stitch with six strands of floss over two threads (see right, "How to Cross-Stitch"). Cut piece ½" around outside of cross-stitching. Cut another piece of cloth the same size. With right sides together and using ¼" seam allowance, sew around all sides, leaving 2" opening for turning. Trim curves and corners and turn. Fill with stuffing and slipstitch opening closed.

NOEL: Work on off-white cloth. When embroidery is complete, assemble ornament according to directions. Whipstitch twisted cording around outside edges of ornament, overlapping ends at center top. From a 10" length of red ribbon, tie a bow and tack in place at overlap. Fold and sew a 6" strand of bright red embroidery floss at top of ornament for hanging loop.

HEART: Work on off-white cloth. When embroidery is complete, assemble ornament according to directions. Whipstitch lace around outside edges of ornament, overlapping raw ends. Fold and sew a 6" strand of off-white embroidery floss at top of ornament for hanging loop.

HOW TO CROSS-STITCH

Use an evenweave fabric. To prevent raveling, zigzag or whipstitch raw edges. Place fabric in an embroidery hoop to keep taut while stitching. To avoid creases, do not leave work in hoop when not stitching. Cut floss into 18" lengths; separate to number of strands specified. Use an embroidery or tapestry needle. Do not knot your thread.

Each cross-stitch is made over the intersection of one lengthwise and one crosswise thread on the fabric. Always pass the needle through the "holes," not the threads. Begin by bringing needle up through fabric, leaving a 1" strand of floss on back. Hold this strand in the direction you are stitching; secure by stitching over it.

The cross-stitch is made in two steps: You form an "X" by passing the floss diagonally across the fabric threads in two directions (A). Be sure all 1–2 stitches are underneath, and all 3–4 stitches are on top. When making a row of adjacent stitches in the same color, work the 1–2 stitches of the "X" the required number of times, then work back, "crossing" all the stitches with 3–4 top stitches (B). When making adjacent stitches, pass the needle through the same hole more than once. To secure end of floss, slide the needle under several stitches on the back of work and snip excess floss.

Each symbol on a chart represents one cross-stitch; different symbols represent different colors. Do not carry floss across back from one color area to another.

WREATH: Work on red cloth. When embroidery is complete, assemble ornament according to directions. Whipstitch twisted cording around outside edges of ornament, overlapping ends at center top. Cut a 10" piece of red ribbon, tie into a bow, and tack in place at overlap. Fold and sew a 6" strand of bright red embroidery floss at top of ornament for hanging loop.

SNOWFLAKE #1: Work on off-white cloth. When embroidery is complete, assemble ornament according to directions. Whipstitch lace around outside edges of ornament, overlapping raw ends. Fold and sew a 6" strand of off-white embroidery floss at one corner of ornament for hanging loop.

SNOWFLAKE #2: Work on off-white cloth. When embroidery is complete, assemble ornament according to directions. Whipstitch lace around outside edges of ornament, overlapping raw ends. Fold and sew a 6" strand of off-white embroidery floss at center of one side of ornament for hanging loop.

SNOWFLAKE #3: Work on red cloth. When embroidery is complete, assemble ornament according to directions. Whipstitch lace around outside edges of ornament, overlapping raw ends. Fold and sew a 6" strand of off-white embroidery floss at center of one side of ornament for hanging loop.

▪ *Sampler Ornament Charts*

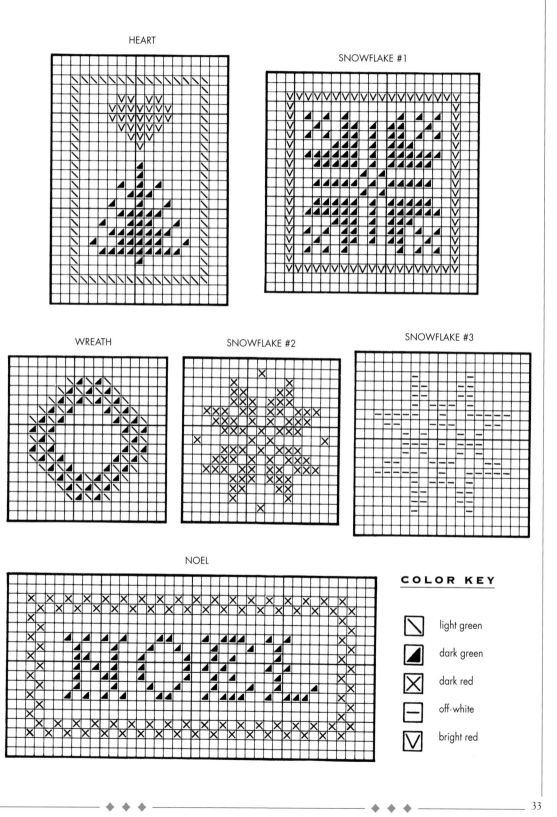

EACH SQUARE = 2 THREADS

HEART

SNOWFLAKE #1

WREATH

SNOWFLAKE #2

SNOWFLAKE #3

NOEL

COLOR KEY

◢	light green
◢	dark green
✕	dark red
—	off-white
V	bright red

WOODEN ANGELS

Sophisticated yet whimsical, these flying angels add a heavenly touch to any decor. Displayed on a mantel or tabletop, this trio of trumpeting angels heralds the holidays with style.

If you don't have a jigsaw, ask a friend who has one to cut out the shapes provided. The painting is easy, but if the colors shown don't fit in with your color scheme, they can be altered to suit your tastes.

SIZE

- Each angel is 7" tall x 14" long.

YOU WILL NEED

FOR THREE ANGELS WITH BASES:
- 4 ft length ¾" x 8" clear pine for angels
- 4 ft length 1" x 8" #2 grade pine for bases and brace
- 2 ft length ¼" diameter dowel
- 2 oz squeeze bottles acrylic paint in red, blue, gold, white, and green
- 2 gold markers, medium point and fine point
- Spray adhesive and wood glue
- Medium and fine sandpapers and tack cloth
- Spring clamps and 1" screws
- Drill and jigsaw
- ½" flat paintbrush and small sponge
- Metal ruler, tracing paper, transfer paper, and pencil

DIRECTIONS

NOTE: Let paints dry completely between steps.

CUTTING: Enlarge and trace three angel and six arm patterns onto tracing paper (see page 16, "Enlarging Patterns"). Spray the back of each pattern piece with spray adhesive and attach to ¾" x 8" pine. With jigsaw, cut out one angel body and two arms for each angel. Mark edge of angel for drill hole with pencil. Side angels will have angled drill holes and center angel will have a vertical drill hole.

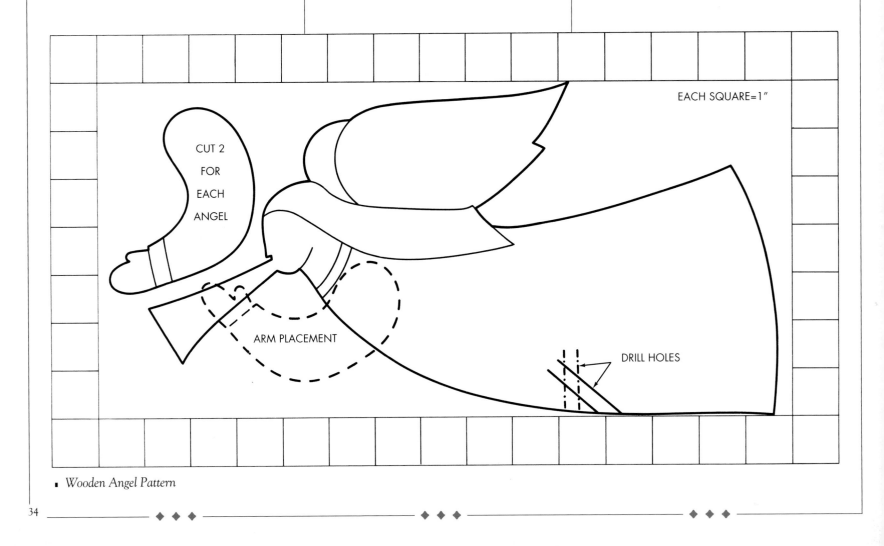

EACH SQUARE=1"

CUT 2 FOR EACH ANGEL

ARM PLACEMENT

DRILL HOLES

- *Wooden Angel Pattern*

Remove paper pattern. Cut two pieces of 1" x 8" pine approximately 13" long. Place the 13" edge of one piece flush with and perpendicular to the surface of the other, and screw together to make an L-shaped brace for drilling. Place one angel inside brace, resting wing and trumpet on base and flat surface against upright board, and clamp in place. Drill 1" hole in edge at angle marked. Repeat for remaining angels. Cut two pieces of dowel 7" long for side angels and one piece 5" long for center angel. Cut three rectangles, 4"x6", for bases from remaining 1" x 8" pine. Sand pieces and round edges with both grades of sandpaper. Wipe with tack cloth.

PAINTING: Paint all dowels and bases gold. Put transfer paper, carbon side down, on angel body. Lay body pattern on top of transfer paper and trace shape with pencil. Transfer pattern to both sides of all angels. Repeat for arm pieces. Glue arms onto bodies, where marked, holding together pieces with clamps until they are thoroughly dry. If desired, colored paints can be mixed with a little white paint. Edges of shapes should be painted to match flat surfaces. Wet sponge and dab in small amount of red, blue, or green paint—center angel should be painted red, and side angels should be painted blue and green. Wipe color onto dress area of angels, allowing wood grain to show through. Paint hands, face, and trumpet with gold, using paintbrush and covering wood completely. Paint wings and hair white. Using gold markers and following photograph, draw decorative details on dress and hair areas.

ASSEMBLY: Glue dowel into each angel. Glue angels onto base.

FATHER CHRISTMAS

Find a special spot by your tree for this folksy Father Christmas to observe the festivities. This jolly fellow will be a great addition to the family and will join in celebrations for years to come.

His patchwork suit is sewn from fabric scraps, and his hair and beard can be made from either wool roving or polyester stuffing.

SIZE
- Finished doll is 25" tall.

YOU WILL NEED
- 1 yd white muslin
- 1 yd quilted white muslin
- 2 gray buttons, $1/2$" diameter, for eyes
- 1 white pompom
- Polyester stuffing
- White wool roving or polyester stuffing for hair
- Small amounts each contrasting light and dark red and green calico fabrics
- Small amount red solid fabric
- 1 skein embroidery floss in white
- Peach-colored pencil
- 1 yd paper-backed fusible web
- Scissors, cardboard, and ruler

DIRECTIONS
NOTE: Clothes are not meant to be removed. It is easier to dress doll before putting on hair and beard. Use $1/4$" seam allowance throughout.

BODY: From white muslin, cut two $7^1/2$"x $9^1/2$" body pieces. Enlarge pattern pieces on page 38 (see page 16, "Enlarging Patterns"), and cut two head pieces. Cut four leg pieces and four arm pieces, reversing two of each.

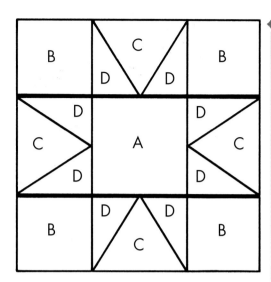

■ *Father Christmas Piecing Diagram*

Cut one nose piece. With right sides together, sew around four sides of body, leaving 3" opening for turning. Trim seams, clip corners, and turn right side out. Stuff with polyester stuffing and whipstitch opening closed. With right sides together, sew around two leg pieces, leaving 3" opening for turning. Trim seams, clip corners, and turn. Fill with polyester stuffing and whipstitch opening closed. Repeat for second leg. Whipstitch legs to lower edge of body, with feet facing out. With right sides together, sew around two arm pieces, leaving 3" opening for turning. Trim seams, clip corners, and turn. Fill with polyester stuffing and whipstitch opening closed. Repeat for second arm. Whipstitch arms to upper edge of body, with arms slanting down. With right sides together, sew around two head pieces, leaving 3" opening for turning. Trim seams, clip corners, and turn. Fill with polyester stuffing and whipstitch opening closed. Whipstitch head to top of body. Press nose piece $\frac{1}{8}$" to wrong side around all edges. Holding a small piece of polyester stuffing between nose and face so nose bulges, center nose on face and slipstitch in

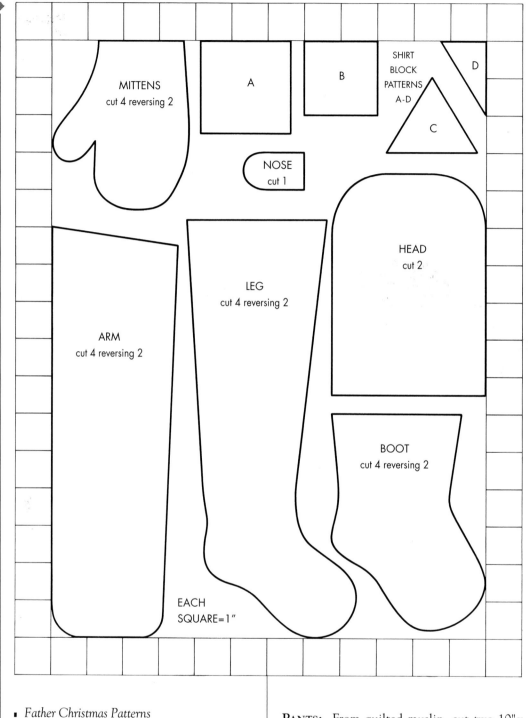

■ *Father Christmas Patterns*

place. Sew on gray buttons for eyes. Using peach-colored pencil, lightly shade face.

PANTS: From quilted muslin, cut two 10"x 12" rectangles for pant pieces. With right sides together, sew along both long edges. Mark 5" on one short edge of both pieces. At this mark, cut 6" toward center, perpendicular to short end, dividing for legs. Sew front and back together along this cut for inner leg seams. Cut two pieces of light red calico, 1½" x 10", and two strips of fusible web, 1" x 10". Press calico ¼" to wrong side along edges. Following manufacturer's instructions, fuse web to wrong side of each piece of calico. Fuse calico in place around lower edge of each pant leg, covering raw edges and overlapping ends. Using six strands of embroidery floss and running stitches, gather waist edge of pants. Place pants on body and tie embroidery thread into bow to secure.

SHIRT: From quilted muslin, cut two 9" x 11" rectangles for shirt front and back and two 5" x 9" rectangles for sleeves. With right sides together, sew front to back along one short edge for shoulders. Press seams open. Folding piece at shoulder seam, cut a semicircle, 1" deep and 5" wide, on front and back of shirt piece for neck. Open shirt piece flat. With right sides together, pin long edge of sleeve at each side edge with shoulder seam at center of sleeve. Sew in place. Cut two pieces of dark red calico, 1½" x 9", and two strips of fusible web, 1" x 9". Press calico ¼" to wrong side along edges. Following manufacturer's instructions, fuse web to wrong side of each piece of calico. Fold calico pieces in half lengthwise and fold over raw edges of each sleeve. Fuse in place, overlapping ends. Cut a bias strip from dark red calico, 1½" x 12", and a strip of fusible web, 1" x 12". Press calico ¼" to wrong side along edges. Following manufacturer's instructions, fuse web to wrong side of calico piece. Fuse calico in place around neck edge as for sleeve binding, overlapping ends.

PATCHWORK: From dark green calico, cut out one A piece. From dark red calico, cut out four

B pieces. From light red calico and light green calico, cut out two C pieces each. From white muslin, cut out eight D pieces. Following piecing diagram at left, sew patchwork pieces together. Press seams flat. Press ¼" to wrong side on outer edges. Using embroidery floss and running stitches, following photograph, sew along all edges of patchwork square. Cut a piece of fusible web 5" x 5". Following manufacturer's instructions, fuse web onto wrong side of patchwork square. Fuse patchwork square in center of shirt front. Sew side and sleeve seams. Cut a piece of light red calico, 1½" x 22", and a strip of fusible web, 1" x 22". Press calico ¼" to wrong side along edges. Following manufacturer's instructions, fuse web to wrong side of calico piece. Fuse calico in place at lower edge of shirt as for pants binding, covering raw edges and overlapping ends. Place shirt on body.

HAIR: Pull clumps of roving or polyester stuffing for hair and tack in place as desired over head and face.

HAT: From quilted muslin, cut a 6" diameter semicircle for hat. Folded with right sides together to make a quarter-circle, sew seam along straight edge to make a cone shape. Turn right side out. Cut a piece of dark red calico, 1½" x 12", and a strip of fusible web, 1" x 12". Press calico ¼" to wrong side along edges. Following manufacturer's instructions, fuse web to wrong side of calico piece. Fuse calico in place at lower edge of hat as for pants binding, overlapping ends. Sew pompom in place at top of hat. Tack hat in place on doll's head.

BOOTS: From dark green calico, cut four pattern pieces, reversing two. With right sides together, sew around each boot, leaving top edge open. Trim seams and turn right side out.

Fold top edge ¼" to wrong side and sew in place. Slide boots over feet and tack in place.

MITTENS: From solid red fabric, cut four pattern pieces, reversing two. With wrong sides together and using six strands of embroidery floss, blanket stitch (see below, "How to Blanket Stitch") edges of each mitten, leaving wrist open. Fold top edge ¼" to wrong side. Using running stitch and embroidery floss, sew in place. Stuff mitten with polyester stuffing. Tack a mitten on end of each arm.

HOW TO BLANKET STITCH

The stitch is worked from left to right. Beginning at outer edge of fabric (1), bring the needle from back of fabric to front. Insert needle above and slightly to the right (2) and bring it out immediately below, drawing the needle through, over the working thread (3). The needle is inserted again at inside a little further along, emerging below at outside edge, drawn over the working thread.

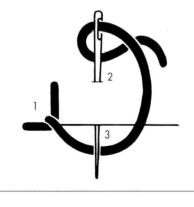

COUNTING TIME

Since before Christian times, the month of December has been a season during which people counted days. The winter solstice, which brings the shortest day of the year, occurs only a few days before Christmas on December 21. Pagan folks anticipated and celebrated the winter solstice with joy and optimism—for them it meant that the days would be getting longer. The decorative use of evergreens also dates back to ancient times. During the bleak and colorless days of winter, greens were brought indoors as a symbol of ever-renewing life and the return of spring.

COUNTING-THE-DAYS ADVENT CALENDAR

Start a family tradition with this delightful star-studded fabric advent calendar. It's a project that can involve the whole family—both in making it and in counting the days until Santa's arrival!

As the stars covering the numbers of each date are removed, they can be hung on the tree or strung on a ribbon and used as a garland.

SIZE
- Finished calendar is 25" square.

YOU WILL NEED
- 26" square red print fabric for front
- 27" square red solid fabric for backing
- 20" square green check fabric
- ¼ yd each red, gold, and tan felt
- 26" square fusible batting
- 1 yd paper-backed fusible web
- 2 skeins tan embroidery floss
- 1 skein red embroidery floss
- 4 packages each of red and white medium rickrack
- 25 yellow buttons, each 13mm in diameter
- Embroidery and sewing needles
- Scissors, cardboard, and ruler

DIRECTIONS

CALENDAR: Cut a 20" square of fusible web. Following manufacturer's instructions, fuse web to wrong side of green check fabric. Cut fabric into 25 squares, each 4". Following photograph, fuse squares onto right side of red print fabric, leaving 1" in between each green check square and around outer edges. Fuse web to wrong side of red felt. Cut the numerals 1 through 25 freehand. Fuse numbers, consecutively, in the center of each green check square. Open all 8 packages of rickrack and cut each in half. Pin one end of a piece of white and a piece of red rickrack together and, following photograph, twist lengths to interlock points, keeping edges flat and forming a twist. Make eight twists. Hand sew rickrack twists, evenly spaced, in 1" space between green check squares. Fuse batting to wrong side of front piece. Place front piece, right side up, centered, on wrong side of backing square. Baste from center out to corners and to each edge to secure. With four strands of red floss, sew a button to each square, through all layers, to hold backing in place. Turn ¼" to the wrong side along each edge of

backing, then fold over again to right side of front piece, overlapping corners, and pin in place for border. Slipstitch border in place. Remove basting.

STARS: Trace star piece onto cardboard to use as template. Trace 25 star shapes onto paper backing of fusible web and, following manufacturer's instructions, fuse onto gold felt. Cut out stars, then fuse other side onto tan felt. Cut tan felt along star outline. With three strands of tan floss, work uneven blanket stitch (see page 39, "How to Blanket Stitch") around outside edges of each star. Cut a buttonhole at the center of each star and blanket stitch around buttonhole.

- *Star Template (actual size)*

The Spirit of Giving

HANDMADE GIFTS SEEM TO HAVE SO MUCH MORE MEANING THAN STORE-BOUGHT ONES. WITH THIS GORGEOUS GROUP, WE'VE TRIED TO THINK OF EVERYONE ON YOUR LIST. FOR HARD-TO-SHOP-FOR MEN, WE OFFER UNIQUE HAND-PAINTED TIES AND A DISTINCTIVE TIE CLIP. GIRLS OF ALL AGES WILL LOVE THE EXOTIC CLAY JEWELRY; ANYONE WILL ENJOY THE RIBBON ROSES.

RAINBOW SCARVES AND NECKTIES

A variety of painted textures and patterns adorn this colorful collection of scarves and ties. This technique provides a welcome solution to some of your gift-giving dilemmas this holiday season. Even the man or woman who appears to have everything will treasure a hand-painted necktie or scarf.

Plain, undyed scarves in a variety of sizes and neckties in both silk and polyester can be found in most craft shops.

SIZE

- Neckties, as desired. Scarves, as specified.

YOU WILL NEED

FOR ALL PROJECTS:
- Pots or containers that will not be used for food
- Rubber gloves and paper towels
- Foam paintbrushes, ¾", 1", and 2"
- Round-tip and long-bristle paintbrushes
- Newspapers and plastic wrap to cover work surface

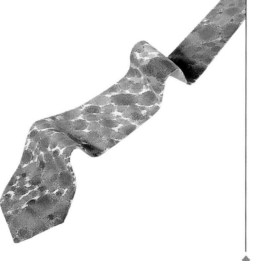

FOR ROYAL BLUE/NATURAL STRIPED NECKTIE:
- 1 undyed silk or polyester necktie
- 2 oz jar water-based silk fabric paint in royal blue

FOR DARK YELLOW/ROYAL BLUE STRIPED NECKTIE:
- 1 undyed silk or polyester necktie
- 2 oz jars water-based silk fabric paint in dark yellow and royal blue

FOR MULTISTRIPED NECKTIE:
- 1 undyed silk or polyester necktie
- 2 oz jars water-based silk fabric paint in plum red, dark yellow, kelly green, cherry red, and black

FOR DARK YELLOW SPOTTED NECKTIE:
- 1 undyed silk or polyester necktie
- 2 oz jars water-based silk fabric paint in dark yellow and royal blue

FOR MULTISPOTTED NECKTIE:
- 1 undyed silk or polyester necktie
- 2 oz jars water-based silk fabric paint in indigo, plum red, and moss green

FOR SPONGE-PAINTED SCARF:
- 30" square undyed silk or polyester scarf
- 2 oz jars water-based silk fabric paint in royal blue, light yellow, and tangerine
- Small natural sponge
- Three-pointed flat tacks
- Wooden artist's stretcher frame, ½" larger than scarf

FOR GEOMETRIC SCARF:

- 36" square undyed silk or polyester scarf
- 2 oz jars water-based silk fabric paint in royal blue, dark yellow, and light yellow
- Three-pointed flat tacks
- Wooden artist's stretcher frame, ½" larger than scarf

FOR DARK YELLOW, ROYAL BLUE, AND WHITE SCARF:

- 30" square undyed silk or polyester scarf
- 2 oz jars water-based silk fabric paint in royal blue and dark yellow
- Three-pointed flat tacks
- Wooden artist's stretcher frame, ½" larger than scarf

FOR COLOR BLOCKS SCARF:

- 8"x 53" undyed silk or polyester scarf
- 2 oz jars water-based silk fabric paint in plum red, dark yellow, turquoise, royal blue, tangerine, and black
- 2 oz jar water-based silk anti-fusant primer
- Three-pointed flat tacks
- Wooden artist's stretcher frame, ½" larger than scarf

FOR BOLD STRIPED SCARF:

- 14"x 58" undyed silk or polyester scarf
- 2 oz jars water-based silk fabric paint in dark yellow and cherry red
- 2 oz jar water-based silk anti-fusant primer
- Three-pointed flat tacks
- Wooden artist's stretcher frame, ½" larger than scarf

FOR SQUIGGLE SCARF:

- 8" x 53" undyed silk or polyester scarf
- 2 oz jars water-based silk fabric paint in royal blue, dark yellow, cherry red, kelly green, turquoise, tangerine, and black
- 2 oz jar water-based silk anti-fusant primer
- Three-pointed flat tacks
- Wooden artist's stretcher frame, ½" larger than scarf

DIRECTIONS

NOTE: Wear rubber gloves when working with paints. Cover work surfaces with newspapers and plastic wrap.

FOR ALL PROJECTS: Following manufacturer's instructions, prepare paint pots for each color. Lay neckties flat on work surface. Rinse scarves in cold water to remove sizing before beginning. Let dry completely. Using three-pointed flat tacks positioned approximately 2" apart, stretch scarves on artist's stretcher frame. Let fabrics dry for 3–5 minutes between steps. The more time paint is allowed to dry, the less the colors will bleed. Paints will bleed into each other in unexpected ways. Paint using fast and even strokes. Following manufacturer's instructions, heat-set fabrics when paint is completely dry.

ROYAL BLUE/NATURAL STRIPED NECKTIE: Using round-tip paintbrush, paint tie with royal blue horizontal stripes, leaving blank spaces between stripes to allow natural color of necktie to show through.

DARK YELLOW/ROYAL BLUE STRIPED NECKTIE: Using round-tip paintbrush, paint tie with dark yellow horizontal stripes, each ½" wide and ¼" apart. Let dry completely. Paint royal blue horizontal lines between dark yellow stripes. Make some lines wider, using more paint in brush, so more bleeds into dark yellow. Make narrow stripes by using less paint.

MULTISTRIPED NECKTIE: Using small long-bristle paintbrush, paint black horizontal stripes approximately 1" to 1½" apart as desired. Let dry completely. Following photograph and using 1" foam paintbrush, paint tie with colors as desired.

DARK YELLOW SPOTTED NECKTIE: Using 2" foam paintbrush, paint entire tie with an even coat of dark yellow. Let dry for approximately 5 minutes. Using small round-tip paintbrush, paint small royal blue dots. The wetter the tie, the more pressure put on the brush, and the more paint in the brush, the larger the dots will be.

MULTISPOTTED NECKTIE: Following photograph and using small round-tip paintbrush and all three colors, paint dots in diagonal lines over the entire surface of tie, allowing some of the original color of necktie to show through. The more pressure put on the brush and the more paint in the brush, the larger the dots will be.

SPONGE-PAINTED SCARF: Following photograph and using royal blue, sponge-paint approximately 4" along opposite sides of scarf, allowing natural color to show through as desired. Let dry completely. In same manner and using clean sponge, paint 3½" stripe adjacent to each royal blue stripe with light yellow. Using both light yellow and tangerine

and in same manner, paint 2½" stripe adjacent to each dark yellow stripe. Paint center 7½" with royal blue as for each outside stripe. Let dry completely and remove from frame.

GEOMETRIC SCARF: Using 2" foam paintbrush, paint one-third of scarf with dark yellow and remaining two-thirds with light yellow. Let dry completely. Following photograph and using round-tip paintbrush and royal blue, paint asterisk stars along one side of scarf. Paint two parallel lines, approximately 3" apart, on same side toward center, and fill in with "X"s. Paint large zigzag lines, approximately 4" tall, across same side toward center of scarf. Paint one row of asterisk stars inside one side of zigzag and another row at points of zigzag. Paint two parallel lines, approximately 3" apart, and fill in with vertical lines spaced approximately ¾" apart. Add a second row of large zigzag lines, touching parallel lines. Paint a second row of parallel lines and fill in with diamonds. Paint a third row of large zigzag lines, touching parallel lines, and draw circles in diamonds made and asterisk stars in

between points. Paint parallel lines, approximately 2" apart, and fill in with vertical lines spaced approximately ¾" apart. Finish with a row of asterisk stars. Let dry completely and remove from frame.

DARK YELLOW, ROYAL BLUE, AND WHITE SCARF: Following photograph and using long-bristle paintbrush and dark yellow, paint a stripe along all four sides of scarf, 3" in from each edge, making a square at each corner. Paint corner squares with royal blue. Paint center of scarf with royal blue stripes, approximately 1" apart. Following photograph and using round-tip paintbrush, draw a royal blue squiggly line on each side edge. Paint a dot in each point. Let dry completely and remove from frame.

COLOR BLOCKS SCARF: Following manufacturer's instructions and using 2" foam paintbrush, paint entire scarf with anti-fusant primer. Let dry completely. Using long-bristle paintbrush and black, divide scarf into a grid with each box approximately 3" square. Let dry. Following photograph and using ¾" foam paintbrush, paint each box with different color as desired. Let dry completely and remove from frame.

BOLD STRIPED SCARF: Following manufacturer's instructions and using foam 2" paintbrush, paint entire scarf with anti-fusant primer. Let dry completely. Following photograph and using 2" foam paintbrush, paint scarf with 2" wide stripes, alternating dark yellow and cherry red. Leave small spaces between stripes, crosswise and parallel to short ends of scarf. Let dry completely and remove from frame.

SQUIGGLE SCARF: Following manufacturer's instructions and using 2" foam paintbrush, paint entire scarf with anti-fusant primer. Let dry completely. Using round-tip paintbrush and colors as desired, paint scarf with squiggly stripes, parallel to short ends of scarf. Let dry completely and remove from frame.

CLAY BEAD JEWELRY

Just about anyone on your Christmas list will love this sophisticated clay jewelry. With these easy-to-learn techniques, you can create jewelry that looks as if it was made in Italy! Follow our directions and adapt them as you wish.

Use the clay in color combinations that will complement current fashions, or choose the upbeat black and white version, which will always look sharp.

JEWELRY SETS

- Black and White Set includes a necklace, earrings, a bracelet, and a barrette.
- Jewel Tone Set includes a necklace, earrings, a bracelet, a barrette, and a pin.

YOU WILL NEED

FOR ALL JEWELRY:
- Plastic brayer (roller), craft knife, and ruler
- Baking sheet, metal skewers, and needle-nosed pliers
- Hot-glue gun and glue sticks
- Black leather cord for necklaces
- Barrette backing
- Silver or gold ear-wires and findings
- Black or silver heavy cord elastic

FOR BLACK AND WHITE SET:
- 2 packages each polymer clay in black and white
- Small amount each polymer clay in dark red, magenta, and green for cat barrette
- Small amount black felt for cat barrette
- Small cat cookie cutter for cat barrette
- 1 package each silver beads in small, medium, and large

- Necklace clasp
- 2 looped-head pins

FOR JEWEL TONE SET:
- 1 package each polymer clay in red, blue, green, white, and magenta
- Pin backing
- 1 package small gold beads
- 1 package silver ring beads
- 2 looped-head pins

DIRECTIONS

NOTE: Knead clay to soften. If clay becomes too soft, harden by storing in the freezer until it becomes firm. Wash hands when changing colors. To avoid fingerprints, handle pieces as little as possible. Use sharp craft knife to cut clay and make cuts clean and smooth. When making holes in beads, push skewer through completely to make a clean hole. Bake beads on skewer to maintain hole. Follow manufacturer's instructions to bake. Let pieces cool completely before handling.

GENERAL DIRECTIONS:

CHECKERBOARD: Using the brayer, roll out same-size slabs, 1/4" thick, of each color. Cut each slab into 1/4" wide strips. Alternating colors, arrange three strips together on flat work surface. Arrange second and third layers of strips, alternating the colors on top of first, until checkerboard brick is 3 strips high and 3 strips wide. Press together with a ruler and secure to make each side flat. Cut checkerboard squares from short end.

MARBLEIZED: Roll two or more colors into ropes. Twist ropes together. Cut in half. Roll and twist ropes together again. Repeat until colors have mixed to desired marbleized pattern.

MILLEFIORI: Make 9 ropes of desired color clay. Arrange 8 around one center rope and press lightly together to make a round core. Roll out a thin slab of outside color and roll around core to encase. Cut off excess and roll together to secure. Cut millefiori slices from short end.

SPIRAL COIL: Using the brayer, roll out same-size slabs, 1/8" thick, of each color. Taper one long edge of each color with fingers. Stack tapered slabs, staggering the pieces as you would a jelly roll. Roll the slabs, starting on the tapered edge. Roll together to secure. Cut spiral coil slices from short end.

TWISTED ROPE: Make two ropes in contrasting colors. Hold ropes together at one end and twist other ends to wrap around each other.

WRAPPED ROPE: Make a rope of one color clay for center. Roll out a thin slab of second color and roll around rope to encase. Cut off excess and roll together to secure. Cut wrapped rope slices from short end.

BLACK AND WHITE SET:

CAT BARRETTE: Using brayer, roll a 1/8" thick slab of black. With cat cookie cutter, cut out two cats. Flop one cat to reverse. Cut a small heart from red clay. To make cat's eyes, make a tiny rope of black clay for center. Roll out a thin slab of green and make a tiny wrapped rope. Roll a thin slab of white and make a wrapped rope using black/green wrapped rope as center. Finished rope should be 1/8" diameter. Press gently to make a small oval. Cut four small slices and position as eyes on each cat. Press gently to secure. Roll small dots of magenta clay for cat's noses and place on each cat's face, pressing to secure. Bake cats and heart. Cut piece of felt to cover barrette backing and glue in place. Following photograph, arrange cats and heart on barrette backing and glue in place.

EARRINGS: Make marbleized clay and roll with a brayer until $1/8$" thick. Cut two small triangles with 1" sides. Insert a looped-head pin in one point of each triangle. Make two small oval beads, $1/2$" diameter. Make holes with a head pin. Bake pieces with pins in place. When pieces are cooled, put a small silver bead at each end of head pin on oval bead. Attach ear-wire to one end and triangle to other, using needle-nosed pliers to bend ends to secure.

BRACELET: From white, make one $3/4$" diameter bead. Roll out one black bead $3/8$" diameter and one black bead $5/8$" diameter. With black and white, make a marbleized bead $7/8$" diameter. Make a second marbleized bead $3/4$" diameter and flatten on all sides to form a cube. Make a wrapped rope $1/4$" diameter, with white center and black encasing. Make a small $1/2$" diameter white rope. Cut slices of wrapped rope and cover white rope as desired. Roll rope to decrease size to $1/4$" and distort wrapped rope. Wrap in swirl-like manner around one $3/4$" diameter black bead. Pinch slightly to a barrel shape. Cut thin slices of wrapped rope and arrange around round marbleized bead. Roll to imbed. Arrange wrapped rope slices around center of one white bead as desired. Press gently to secure. With white, make two barrel beads, each 1" long and $3/4$" diameter. Roll checkerboard into rope, $1/2$" diameter, decreasing the size and distorting the checkerboard pattern. Cut thin slices of reduced checkerboard and cover the outside of one barrel bead. Roll bead to imbed. Layer thin strips, of varying thicknesses and $3/4$" wide, of black and white and roll lightly with brayer to

imbed strips. Cut thin slices and wrap around second barrel bead. Roll bead to imbed slices. Make holes in barrel beads through flat end. Make a hole through all nine beads and bake on skewer. When beads are cooled, thread beads on piece of black elastic, alternating clay beads with large silver beads. Tie ends to secure.

NECKLACE: From white, make one bead $1\,1/4$" diameter, two beads $3/4$" diameter, and two cone-shaped beads $1\,1/8$" long. Make a twisted rope with black and white. Wrap piece of twisted rope around each $3/4$" diameter white bead in random manner as desired. Roll to imbed. Make a black rope, $1/8$" thick, and arrange to form two "X"s on each cone-shaped bead. Roll to imbed. From black, make two beads $7/8$" diameter and two beads $5/8$" diameter. Cover $7/8$" diameter beads with small dots of white and roll to imbed. Make two black rings, each $1/8$" thick and $1/2$" diameter. Make $1/8$" diameter rope from white. Wrap with $1/4$" thick black and cut two barrel beads, $1/2$" long. Make holes through round side. Roll remaining wrapped rope until it is $1/8$" diameter, and cut and arrange slices around center of $1\,1/4$" diameter white bead. Roll to imbed. Make marbleized clay rope, $1/8$" thick, and wrap around skewer in spiral manner until a barrel bead, $1\,1/2$" long, has been made. Press spiral layers together to secure. Make two beads in this manner. Make two marbleized barrel beads, each $3/4$" long and $3/4$" diameter. Make holes in flat end. Bake all beads on skewer. When beads are cooled, divide beads evenly. With large $1\,1/4$" bead at center and following photograph, arrange beads as desired. String on leather, alternating clay beads with medium silver beads. Knot leather at beginning and end of beads. Following manufacturer's instructions, attach necklace clasp.

JEWEL TONE SET:

MAKE A MILLEFIORI: Use white center, surrounded by 4 magenta and 4 green ropes and white encasing.

BARRETTE: Cut five thin slices of millefiori. Using brayer, roll a ⅛" thick slab of red clay, then cut a rectangle 1" wide and 3½" long. Arrange and press millefiori slices onto red rectangle. Make a green and white twisted rope and arrange around outside edge of red rectangle. Bake. When pieces are cooled, glue twisted rope to red rectangle to secure. Glue rectangle in place on barrette back.

PIN: Cut one slice of millefiori, ⅛" thick. Make a red rope and arrange around outside edge of millefiori slice. Using brayer, gently press flat to imbed. Make a green and white twisted rope and arrange around outside edge of millefiori-red center. Make a green rope and arrange around outside edge of twisted rope. Bake. When piece is cooled, glue in place on pin backing.

EARRINGS: From red, make two ⅞" diameter beads. Cut two thin slices of millefiori and arrange one on the front of each bead. Roll to imbed. Make holes with a head pin. Bake pieces with pins in place. When pieces are cooled, put a small gold bead at each end of head pin on bead. Attach ear-wire to one end and, using needle-nosed pliers, bend end to secure.

BRACELET: From red, make two ⅞" diameter beads. Cut desired number of slices of millefiori and arrange on one bead. Roll to imbed. From white and green, make spiral coil, ½" diameter. Cut into desired number of slices and arrange around the center of other red bead. From red clay, make a barrel bead, 1" long and ½" diameter. From green and white,

make a twisted rope. Arrange twisted rope around barrel bead. Roll to imbed. Make holes in flat end. Knead green and white clay together to make a light green. Make a ⅞" diameter bead. Cut spiral coil into desired number of slices and arrange randomly around light green bead. Roll to imbed. From white, make a ⅞" diameter bead. Make a magenta rope and arrange in a spiral around white bead. Roll to imbed. Make a marbleized bead from green and blue, ⅝" diameter. Make a marbleized bead from green, blue, and white, ¾" diameter. Cover marbleized beads with small red spots and roll to imbed. Make a marbleized bead from white, magenta, green, and red, ⅝" diameter. Make a wrapped rope with white center, ⅛" diameter, encased in blue, ⅛" thick, and then encased in green, ⅛" thick. Make a barrel bead from wrapped rope, ¾" long and ¾" diameter. Make holes through round side. Make holes through all nine beads and bake on skewer. When beads are cooled, thread on piece of silver elastic, alternating clay beads with silver beads. Tie ends to secure.

NECKLACE: From white, make a 1" diameter bead. Make a green and white spiral coil, ½" diameter, and cover white bead entirely. Roll to imbed. From green, make four beads, ½" diameter. From magenta, make two beads, ½" diameter. From blue, make two beads, ¾" diameter. Make green and white twisted rope and wrap around blue beads as desired. Roll to imbed. From red, make two beads, ¾" diameter. Cover with white spots as desired. Roll to imbed. From white and green, make marbleized clay rope, ¼" thick, and wrap around skewer in spiral manner until barrel bead, 1½" long, has been made. Press spiral layers together to secure. Make two beads in this manner. Make a spiral coil from green and white. Encase with magenta, ⅛" thick. Cut four barrel beads, each ⅝" long from

magenta/green and white spiral. Make holes in rounded edge. Bake all beads on skewer. When beads are cooled, divide evenly. With large 1" bead at center and following photograph, string beads on leather, alternating clay beads with medium silver beads. Knot leather at beginning and end of beads. Knot leather at each end.

Glorious Gifts

What a lovely feeling it is to open up a beautifully wrapped package to discover that the giver has made the gift inside especially for you. Handmade gifts are often treasured long after store-bought items have been forgotten.

Making a handcrafted present doesn't have to be a major undertaking. Choose one of these unique items for someone special on your list:

Ribbon Roses are easy to make and can be used as pins, chokers, hat decorations, garnishes for gift boxes, and much more.

No one can have too many pins and this floral Decoupage Pin will make an unusual addition to anyone's collection. The recipient of this elegant Woven Ribbon Eyeglass Case won't want to hide it in her purse!

And if you are tired of giving endless ties to the men in your life, a quick-to-make Watch Parts Tie Clip is a welcome alternative.

RIBBON ROSES

SIZES

- Finished ribbon rose pins are 2" to 3" wide.

YOU WILL NEED

FOR EACH RIBBON ROSE PIN:
- 1 yd wire-edged ombré ribbon, 1¼" to 1½" wide
- 4 or 5 wire flower stamens
- Paper leaves with wire
- Matching thread
- Pin backing
- Hot-glue gun and glue sticks

DIRECTIONS

For each: Twist wire stamens together for center of rose. Use ¾ yd of ribbon for small and 1 yd for large ribbon rose. Roll one end of ribbon and hem. Attach stamens to beginning stitches. Baste a thread along one long edge. After 1½" has been basted, pull thread to gather and hand-stitch to tack gathers in place. Continue to baste, gather, and tack, rolling ribbon into a spiral circle until all ribbon has been used. Roll end and hem. Following photograph or as desired, attach leaves to base of rose with glue. Glue pin backing in place at back.

DECOUPAGE PIN

SIZE

- Finished pin is 2" square.

YOU WILL NEED

- 2" square of ⅛" thick basswood
- Small flower- and strawberry-patterned gift wrap for cutouts
- 1" square gold filigree
- Black acrylic paint
- Gel medium
- 9" gold trim
- Pin backing
- Acrylic gloss spray sealer
- Craft knife, ruler, and pencil
- Hot-glue gun and glue sticks

DIRECTIONS

Paint 2" square of wood with two coats of black. Cut out four each of white flowers and strawberries. Center gold filigree on painted wood and glue in place. Cover back of flowers and strawberries with gel medium, and follow-ing photograph, place in position, smoothing out air bubbles with fingers as you work. Be sure to cover entire back of each cutout with gel medium and smooth edges to secure. When all motifs are secured, spray with one coat of sealer. Glue gold trim around outside edge of pin square, overlapping ends. Glue pin backing in place on back of square.

WOVEN RIBBON EYEGLASS CASE

SIZE

- Finished case is approximately 4" wide x 8½" long.

YOU WILL NEED

- 1½ yds copper satin ribbon, ⅝" wide
- 1½ yds teal satin ribbon, ⅞" wide
- ½ yd copper metallic lace, 1⅞" wide
- ¼ yd copper satin fabric for lining
- 6" x 9" piece bronze fabric for backing
- 1 ft square corkboard or foam board

- Small snap
- Straight pins, sharp pointed scissors, and thumbtacks

DIRECTIONS

RIBBON WEAVING: Cut one piece of copper fabric, 6" x 9". Attach thumbtack to corkboard, right side up. Cut six pieces of copper ribbon, each 8" long. Cut eight pieces of teal ribbon, each 5" long. Leaving a ½" margin on all sides of copper fabric, tack copper pieces in rows perpendicular to short edge of copper fabric. Tack one end of teal ribbon in place, perpendicular to copper ribbon, and weave under and over copper pieces. Tack other end in place. Repeat for all pieces of teal ribbon. Replace thumbtacks with pins to secure woven ribbons to copper fabric. Remove from corkboard and sew around all sides to secure ends of ribbons to fabric. Trim fabric even with ribbon ends.

ASSEMBLY: Cut a piece of bronze fabric, 5" x 8", for backing. Hold front piece and backing with right sides together. Using ¼" seam allowance, sew around three sides, leaving one short end open; sew along stitching line of woven piece. Turn eyeglass case right side out. Cut one piece of copper lining, 5"x 16". With right sides together, fold lining piece in half crosswise. Sew along both long side edges, leaving top short edge open. Cut one piece of copper lining, 3"x 10", for cuff. Cut one piece of teal ribbon 10" long. Place on cuff piece, ½" in from long raw edge, and topstitch in place. Fold cuff piece in half crosswise, with right sides together. Sew across short edges to form a loop. Turn right side out. Cut one piece of copper lace 10" long. Sew across short edges in same manner as cuff piece to form a loop. Turn right side out. Fold cuff loop in half, right side out, aligning raw edges. Insert cuff loop into

lace loop, aligning raw edges, and topstitch pieces together. Turn wrong side out. Centering seam on back of eyeglass case and aligning raw edges, insert eyeglass case into cuff loop. Using ¼" seam allowance, sew eyeglass case to cuff. Fold open edge of lining ¼" to wrong side and press. Insert lining into eyeglass case and whipstitch open edge to cuff. Sew snap inside eyeglass case on cuff and lining seam.

WATCH PARTS TIE CLIP

SIZE
- Finished clip is 2".

YOU WILL NEED
- Tie clip
- Watch face
- 6" gold trim and half-round gold bead
- Hot-glue gun and glue sticks

DIRECTIONS
Glue gold trim around outside of watch face, overlapping ends. Glue half-round gold bead in center. Glue watch face to tie clip.

Bow-and-Star Pullover and Patchwork Vest

Two perfect clothing gifts to make for special ladies on your Christmas list are the Bow-and-Star Pullover and Patchwork Vest. Both styles are versatile enough to be worn for dressy or casual occasions.

The red Bow-and-Star Pullover will look stunning with a simple skirt or slacks and would be equally appropriate for at-home entertaining or holiday evenings out. The lush green satin bow on the shoulder is the perfect Christmas touch to a celestial theme.

Patchwork squares are blanket stitched onto a man's vest "borrowed" from Dad's closet or purchased from a thrift shop. We've used cotton print fabric scraps left over from other Christmas projects. A more dressy look could be achieved by using lush velvets or brocades.

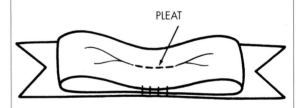

PLEAT

- *Bow Diagram for Bow-and-Star Pullover*

BOW-AND-STAR PULLOVER

SIZE

- As desired.

YOU WILL NEED

- Red sweater
- 1 yd green satin
- Matching thread
- 11 star charms
- Scissors, pins, cardboard, and ruler

DIRECTIONS

BOW: From green satin, cut three 8½" wide bias strips, one 5" long, one 22" long, and one 30" long. With right sides together, fold strips in half lengthwise and pin. Using ¼" seam allowance, sew the 5" and 30" strips along long edge. Turn right side out and press flat with seam at center of back of strips. Turn under one end of 5" strip for bow center and press. Fold 30" strip in half to make a 14" loop for bow, overlapping ends at center. Sew long edge of 22" strip for streamers, leaving a 5" opening at center for turning. Do not turn but position seam at center back as before and pin at ends; do not press folds. Mark a 2" deep "V" at each end and stitch. Clip points and cut "V". Turn right side out, pushing out points. Press and slipstitch opening closed. Place the 14" loop bow wrong side up on table. Handling all layers as one, fold in half lengthwise, aligning long edges. At the center, make a 2" long seam parallel to and about 1" from the fold, forming a pleat. Unfold and press pleat flat. Center bow on streamers and tack in place. Place raw edge of 5" bow center on wrong side of bow at 2" pleat. Wrap 5" strip around bow, covering raw end. Slipstitch center strip in place, catching in bow as you stitch.

PULLOVER PLACEMENT: Following photograph, pin bow at shoulder and arrange star charms on sweater as desired. Sew in place.

PATCHWORK VEST

SIZE

- As desired.

YOU WILL NEED

- Man's vest
- Small amounts each assorted red, green, and white cotton fabrics
- 1 skein each embroidery floss in off-white and red
- 1 yd paper-backed fusible web
- Matching thread and embroidery needle
- 12 gold buttons and assorted gold charms
- Scissors, pins, cardboard, and ruler

DIRECTIONS

Cut fabric into 36 pieces, each 2" square. Following photograph, arrange 9 squares to make a patchwork block. Using ¼" seam allowance, sew the squares together in rows, then sew the rows together. Repeat with 9 more squares. Press ¼" to wrong side around all sides of blocks. Press seams flat. Following manufacturer's instructions, fuse web to wrong side of each block. With six strands of off-white embroidery floss, blanket stitch around outside edge of each block. Fuse one block to each side of front of vest in desired position. Fuse web to wrong side of remaining 18 squares. With six strands of red embroidery floss, blanket stitch (see page 39, "How to Blanket Stitch") around each square. Arrange 9 squares on each side of front of vest, overlap-

ping some as desired. Fuse in place. Replace original vest buttons with gold buttons. Scatter and sew remaining buttons and assorted charms around vest. With six strands of off-white embroidery floss, work running stitches along entire edge of each side of front.

BEAUTIFUL BOXES

A unique handmade box makes a splendid gift on its own or as a container for a gift within a gift. And no one can have too many boxes, whether for storing jewelry, hiding odds and ends, or simply as a conversation piece on a coffee table or desktop.

Our collection includes boxes decorated with a variety of techniques. The Red-Paper Holiday Box is covered in marbleized paper with wrapping paper accents, while the Plaid Band Box is covered in a striking silk shantung fabric. Whimsical paper cutouts form a tree pattern on the Decoupage Box, and a delicate sun and star motif adorns the Celestial Box. Easy-to-create wood-grain patterns make a handsome Faux Inlay Box.

SIZES

- Red-Paper Holiday Box is 6½" wide x 5" deep x 3" high. Plaid Band Box is 10" diameter x 4" high. Decoupage Box is 8" wide x 5" deep x 3" high. Celestial Box is 7" wide x 6" deep x 3" high. Faux Inlay Box is 10¾" wide x 4" deep x 3" high.

YOU WILL NEED

FOR ALL BOXES:
- Spray adhesive and acrylic clear spray sealer
- Craft knife, ruler, newspaper, and pencil

FOR RED-PAPER HOLIDAY BOX:
- Rectangular box
- 1 piece each red marbleized and green holly/gold gift wrap

FOR PLAID BAND BOX:
- Round papier-mâché band box
- ½ yd silk shantung plaid fabric
- Gold acrylic paint
- 1" foam paintbrush

FOR DECOUPAGE BOX:
- Rectangular box
- Gold acrylic paint
- Paper cutouts in desired motifs
- Gel medium
- Basting adhesive
- 1" foam paintbrush

FOR CELESTIAL BOX:
- Oval band box
- Acrylic paint in dark blue, light blue, and gold
- Stiff-bristle artist's paintbrush, 1" flat paintbrush, and sponge
- Gold marker
- Paper plate, tracing paper, ball point, and soft lead pencil

FOR FAUX INLAY BOX:
- Rectangular hinged box
- 2 oz bottles wood stain in maple, mahogany, golden oak, and cherry
- Paper plate, paper towels, plastic fork, and cotton swabs
- ¾" masking tape, small sponge, and ½" flat paintbrush

DIRECTIONS

NOTE: Cover work surface with newspaper. Let paints and sealers dry completely between steps.

RED-PAPER HOLIDAY BOX: Using box as a pattern, lay each side of box lid on red paper and trace. With craft knife, cut out paper ¼" larger than tracing on the bottom edge and one end. For top of lid, cut paper ¼" larger on all sides. Spray wrong side of each piece of paper and outside of box with spray adhesive. Beginning with top of lid, lay paper, centered, on box and press paper on box to secure, smoothing out bubbles with fingers as you work. Fold ¼" excess down each side. Clip around hinges and at corners of paper on lid. Work side pieces in same manner, folding excess to side without paper and lining up cut edge with top of box lid. On last side, trim paper to fit exactly. Work box in same manner beginning with bottom. Cut four strips of green holly/gold paper, each ½" wide and the

■ *Faux Inlay Box (above)*

length of each side edge of box lid. Spray wrong side with spray adhesive and place ½" down from top of lid, along each side. Cut four strips of green holly/gold paper, each ½" wide and the length of each top edge of box lid. Spray wrong side with spray adhesive and place ½" inside edges of box lid, overlapping in corners. Cut diamond shape from green holly/gold paper to fit inside borders of box lid. Spray wrong side with spray adhesive and smooth in place on box lid. Spray with two coats of sealer.

PLAID BAND BOX: Paint inside of box gold. Measure the height and circumference of the outside of box. Cut a strip of fabric as wide as and ½" longer than circumference of box. Trace bottom of box on wrong side of fabric and cut out. Trace top of lid of box on wrong side of fabric and cut out ¼" larger. Measure the height and circumference of the outside of box lid. Cut a strip of fabric as wide as and ½" longer than circumference of box lid. Spray outside surfaces of box and wrong side of fabric pieces with spray adhesive. Center lid on matching fabric piece. Press to secure, smoothing out air bubbles with fingers as you work. Clip excess fabric every ½". Fold excess fabric to side of box lid, overlapping clipped fabric to ease fit. Cover sides of lid with fabric strip, turning one end ¼" to wrong side and overlapping ends. Press to secure. Center box bottom on corresponding fabric piece. Press to secure, smoothing out air bubbles with fingers. Cover sides of box bottom as for box lid.

DECOUPAGE BOX: Paint inside and outside of box with two coats of gold paint. Using basting adhesive, arrange cutouts as desired. Remove and cover back of each motif with gel medium and place in position, smoothing out air bubbles with fingers as you work. Be sure to cover entire back of motifs with gel medium and smooth edges down to secure. If images overlap, work on bottom images first. When all cutouts are secured, spray box with two coats of sealer.

CELESTIAL BOX: Paint outside of box and lid dark blue. Paint inside of box gold. In paper plate, squeeze out all three colors of paint, one on top of the other, forming concentric circles. Dip sponge in layered paint in paper plate. Lightly sponge-paint top of box lid and outside edges of box. Try not to mix paints in order to keep a marbleized effect. Make transfer paper by rubbing a soft lead pencil to cover entire side of tracing paper. Put transfer paper, penciled side down, on top of box lid. Trace sun and star motif (see page 66) onto tracing paper. Lay sun and star pattern on center of box lid over transfer paper. With ball point, outline design on box lid. Remove transfer paper and pattern. With gold marker, draw over transfer lines of design. Add small stars around central motif. Following photograph, make some stars "shooting stars" and some "bright stars." Continue to draw stars on side edges of box. When design is complete, spray with two coats of sealer.

■ *Plaid Band Box (left); Red-Paper Holiday Box (above left); Decoupage Box (above right)*

FAUX INLAY BOX:

NOTE: Masking tape is used to mark off design and keep painting lines crisp and clean. Run a finger along tape to attach securely to box so paint won't seep underneath. Do not remove tape until paint is thoroughly dry. Paper plate will be used as a palette.

FAUX INLAY: Following photograph, run a length of tape along each side edge of top of lid, overlapping corners. Run a second piece of tape, adjacent to and inside first piece of tape, along short sides of box. Mark a diamond shape in center of inner rectangle. Tape outside edges of diamond. Paint diamond with golden oak stain. While paint is still wet, dab tip of cotton swab in paint to create a bird's-eye maple look. Paint lower part of box in same manner. Remove tape bordering diamond when paint is thoroughly dry. Cover edges of diamond with masking tape to protect. Paint remainder of center rectangle with mahogany. While paint is still wet, pinch fingernails together and, following photograph, pinch and scratch lines in wet paint. When paint is dry, tape inside edges of rectangle to protect. Remove tape along outside edges of box lid, but leave a ¾" square taped in each corner. Paint with cherry. Following photograph and while paint is still wet, use plastic fork to scratch lines crosswise several times around outside edges. When paint is dry, remove tape from inside bars and corners and tape outside edges to protect area just painted. Sponge-paint four corners and two inside bars with maple, allowing some of the natural wood grain to show through. Wash sponge and sponge-paint side of lid with cherry. Dilute small amount of cherry stain with water and, using flat paintbrush, brush over maple sponge-painted section. When paint is dry, spray with two coats of sealer.

■ *Celestial Box Pattern (actual size)*

■ *Celestial Box*

CHRISTMAS COOKING

PART

2

With
Christmas
around the corner,
now is the time for baking
and cooking for the holidays.
Gather in a harvest of your favorite
fruits and vegetables to use for making
cakes and quick breads that will keep well
in the freezer to be enjoyed throughout the holiday
season. Use whatever time you can find to do some cooking,
and tuck the goodies away for later. To get the Christmas season
off to an early and joyous start, have your children help now with the
fun job of cutting cookies and mixing cakes. With a freezer well stocked with
such goodies as homemade Swedish Meatballs, Whole-Wheat Dinner Rolls, and

Southern-Style Sweet
Potato Custard, you
can face the holidays
with confidence. You'll
be well prepared for
entertaining guests at
an elegant dinner party.

Freeze-and-Heat Entrées

MEALS THAT YOU MAKE AND FREEZE ARE THE ULTIMATE IN CONVENIENCE AND HOMEMADE GOODNESS—AND MAKING YOUR OWN COSTS A FRACTION OF THE PRICE OF COMMERCIALLY FROZEN FOODS.

UNDERCOOK PASTAS TO BE FROZEN TO PREVENT THEM FROM HAVING A GUMMY, MUSHY TEXTURE WHEN SERVED. UNFORTUNATELY, MOST DISHES MADE WITH POTATOES,

COOKED RICE, FRIED FOODS, OR CRUMB OR CHEESE TOPPINGS FOR CASSEROLES DON'T FREEZE WELL. (FOR CASSEROLES THAT CALL FOR A TOPPING, MAKE IT AND SPRINKLE IT ON THE CASSEROLE JUST BEFORE BAKING AND SERVING.)

BEFORE PREPARING ANY RECIPE IN THIS CHAPTER, READ "SUCCESSFUL FREEZING" ON PAGE 72.

FREEZING FACTS

- Start with the freshest, highest quality foods to freeze. Freezing will maintain food's quality, but can't improve it.
- Prepare food in sanitary conditions before freezing. Keep work surfaces, equipment, and utensils clean throughout the preparation process.
- Use freezer-safe wrap or containers that are moisture- and vapor-proof to prevent freezer burn and to protect food's nutrients.
- Label the packages well with the type of food, quantity or number of servings, date made, and expiration date.
- Cool food quickly in the refrigerator before placing it in the freezer.
- Don't overload the freezer: freeze no more than two to three pounds of food per cubic foot of space at any one time.
- Until foods are frozen solid, do not let the sides of the packages touch each other. This will allow cold air to get to all the surfaces for more successful freezing. After 24 hours, you can stack the frozen packages.
- Let the freezer do its job—keep the door closed. When adding or removing items from the freezer, open the door as briefly as possible.
- Be sure the temperature in the freezer is 0°F or colder. If your freezer doesn't have a thermostat with temperature, use a special freezer thermometer.
- Remember the "First In/First Out" rule. Rotate and use your frozen foods within their optimal time to ensure best quality in taste, appearance, texture, and nutrition.

SUCCESSFUL FREEZING

The two most important elements in successful food freezing are wrapping and temperature.

WRAP IT RIGHT

The purpose of freezer wrap and containers is to prevent food from drying out and to preserve its nutrition, flavor, texture, and color. Therefore, the wrap or container you use should be moisture- and vapor-proof, should be easy to push air out of, and should seal tightly. The wrap or container should be odorless and tasteless as well. Read manufacturers' labels to be sure the material you plan to use is recommended for freezing.

Rigid containers are those made of plastic or glass with tight-fitting lids that can be stacked in the freezer. These are especially useful for freezing liquids and very moist foods, such as jams, sauces, chili, and frostings. If you opt for glass containers, use those that have wide mouths and slightly slanting sides and are approved for freezing.

Liquids expand when frozen, so leave space at the top to allow for expansion—½ inch for pints and 1 inch for quarts or for wide-mouth containers—or the food will rise up and knock the lid off.

When you freeze in most microwave-safe plastic or freezer-proof/heat-tempered glass, you can take your food directly from the freezer and heat it in the microwave oven.

Flexible wrap includes heavy-duty aluminum foil, white freezer wrap, plastic wrap for freezing, and freezer bags—do not use lightweight sandwich bags or waxed paper. Freezer wraps are good for small, loose foods, such as cookies, meatballs, or stuffed pasta shells, or foods with irregular shapes, such as loaves of bread, casseroles, or stacks of crepes.

SERVING MADE EASY

While you're wrapping food for freezing, consider how you will defrost and heat it. Use wrapping techniques that will make your life easier when it's time to serve the food you've frozen. Here are some options for wrapping to help make serving easy:

- When freezing casseroles, you can put the cold food—whether cooked or not—directly in freezer-to-oven-to-table casserole dishes, wrap well, label, and freeze. (Many nonmetal freezer-safe dishes can go directly into the microwave oven.)
- If you're short on casserole dishes, freeze in heavy aluminum foil pans that can be reused or disposed of after the food is served.
- A very handy tip is to line a freezer-safe casserole dish with heavy-duty aluminum foil, then freeze the casserole in the foil-lined dish until hard. Remove the frozen casserole from the dish, wrap it well, label it, and return the food to the freezer without the dish. (If the food you are freezing contains an acid, such as tomatoes, put a layer of plastic wrap between the food and the foil. The acid can react with foil during storage.) When serving the casserole, thaw it just until you can remove the foil and plastic wrap, if used. Put the partially frozen food in the same casserole dish in which it was frozen and heat it, thoroughly, to 165°F.

- Give yourself options in serving sizes, too. If you're making a big batch of soup, for example, freeze some of it in quart-size containers that will serve four and freeze some of it in 8-ounce containers for single servings. Freeze crepes, pasta sauces, and casseroles, too, with serving size options in mind.
- Take special care with fragile frozen foods, such as pie crusts, unfilled cream puffs, and baked cookies. Wrap those items in flexible wrap first, then put them in boxes or rigid containers. Avoid stacking heavy frozen foods on top of them.

SEAL IT AIRTIGHT

Making an airtight seal on flexible wrap is essential:

- For self-sealing freezer bags, which come in quart and gallon sizes, simply squeeze out as much air as possible, then zip closed.
- For foil wrap, seal the edges by pulling two edges together and folding them over two or three times or until the fold is flat against the top of the food. Fold the ends over several times also to seal the package airtight.
- For white freezer wrap and plastic wrap for freezing, seal the package in the same way as described for foil wrap, then tape all the edges very well with tape made especially for freezing. Don't even think about using masking tape. It won't stay "stuck."

LABEL EVERYTHING

Labeling your food for the freezer is as important as wrapping it well. If your wrapping material can be written on with a waterproof marker, you can write the name of the food, amount enclosed, and the date and expiration date directly on the wrap. If the material will not accept the marker, write on a piece of freezer tape, then stick it to the package.

TEMPERATURE IS VITAL

The storage life indicated at the end of the recipes in this chapter assumes that the freezer temperature is 0°F or colder. The storage life will be less if your freezer is warmer.

Food stored longer than the times indicated in the recipes will still be safe to eat, but the quality will not be as good.

If you don't own a freestanding freezer and would like to stock foods you've made or take advantage of bargains from the market, consider renting freezer space from a local locker.

The method of freezing suggested in some of the recipes that follow—freezing food unwrapped just until frozen solid—helps to avoid excess moisture getting trapped between the food and the wrap.

NOTE: While freezing and storage information is given for all the recipes in this section, you can prepare any of them to cook and serve immediately. You may need to adjust cooking times on some recipes.

TAKING INVENTORY

Keeping track of your freezer's contents is like running a small store—you must know what you have, where it is, how long it's been there, and its "use-by" date. For stocking up on Christmas specials, it's also nice to have a record of your intended uses for the foods you've put away in the freezer.

With all your packages and containers clearly labeled with contents, quantity, and date, you have a head start on identifying foods. It also helps you keep foods of similar types together.

Take an inventory and keep the list inside a cupboard door or near your freezer where you can easily add and subtract the items you put in and take out of the freezer. A chalkboard works well. Your list might look like this:

ITEM	DATE MADE	QUANTITY MADE	QUANTITY REMOVED	USE WITHIN	PLANS
Broccoli-Cheese Quiche	10/7	4 quiches		6 weeks	birthday brunch
Swedish Meatballs	10/7	3 one-doz. bags	2 one-doz. bags	3 months	family meals
Swedish Carlquist Cardamom Bread	11/15	2 loaves		3 months	tree-trimming party
Aunt Snookum's Chocolate Pound Cake	11/16	1 tube cake		6 months	tree-trimming party (drizzle with Hot Fudge Sauce)
Gingerbread People	11/30	4 one-doz. bags		6 months	Christmas Eve drop-ins
Prune Quick Bread	12/1	2 loaves		3 months	basket for Franklins

BROCCOLI-CHEESE QUICHE

Garnish this green-flecked quiche with cut cherry tomatoes and parsley and serve as a first course for a dinner party or as an entrée with apple, grape, and pecan salad and steamed carrots for brunch or lunch.

PASTRY:

1 recipe (4 single crusts) Penny's Never-Fail Pie Crust (see page 119)

FILLING:

16 eggs

½ teaspoon salt

½ teaspoon ground nutmeg

⅛ teaspoon white or black pepper

7 cups milk, half-and-half, or light cream

2 packages (10 ounces each) frozen chopped broccoli, thawed and drained, or 4 cups chopped fresh broccoli, blanched

1 pound shredded Cheddar or Swiss cheese (4 cups)

TO MAKE THE PASTRY: Make pie crust according to recipe. Form into 4 equal balls; wrap and refrigerate for at least 1 hour. Preheat the oven to 425°F. Roll out 1 pastry ball to a 12-inch circle on a lightly floured board. Fold into quarters and fit into a 9-inch pie plate or a disposable pie pan. Cover with foil. Fill the pastry with uncooked rice or beans to prevent the pastry from bubbling as it bakes. Repeat with the remaining 3 pastry balls.

Bake for 5 to 7 minutes, or until firm but not brown. Remove from the oven and let cool slightly on a wire rack. Remove weights and foil.

TO MAKE THE FILLING: Reduce the oven temperature to 325°F. In a large bowl, beat the eggs lightly. Stir in the salt, nutmeg, pepper, and milk or cream. Pour the mixture through a fine strainer.

In each pie crust, sprinkle 1 cup chopped broccoli and 1 cup cheese. Measure 2¾ cups egg mixture and pour over broccoli and cheese in each pie crust. (If you can bake only 2 at a time, fill only 2 crusts to be baked and refrigerate remaining filling until ready to bake.)

TO BAKE: Bake for 35 to 40 minutes, or until a knife inserted near the center comes out clean. Remove quiches from the oven and cool for 1 hour on wire racks before freezing.

TO FREEZE: To protect the pie and fragile side crusts, place an inverted paper plate over the top of each quiche and tape the edges of the paper plate to the pie plate, to secure it. Wrap each quiche individually with flexible freezer wrap and seal. Label and freeze for up to 6 weeks.

TO SERVE: Preheat the oven to 375°F. Unwrap the quiche and cover the edges with foil to prevent over-browning. Bake frozen quiche for 50 minutes, or until heated through. (Do not reheat quiche in a microwave oven.)

Makes 4 quiches (each serves 6 as an entrée or 10 as an appetizer)

VARIATIONS: Instead of the cheese, add 4 cups small cooked shrimp, 4 cups chopped cooked ham, or 4 cups sliced fresh mushrooms sautéed in 2 tablespoons margarine or butter. Or, omit the nutmeg and add 2 teaspoons snipped fresh tarragon or ¾ teaspoon dried tarragon, crushed.

For appetizer quiches: Roll 1 pastry ball into a 16-inch square. Cut out 24 2½-inch circles, re-rolling the dough, as necessary. Line 24 1¾-inch muffin cups with pastry. For filling, beat together 2 eggs, dash of salt, dash of ground nutmeg, and ¾ cup milk, half-and-half, or light cream; set aside. Divide ¾ cup chopped, cooked broccoli and ¾ cup shredded Cheddar cheese among the pastry-lined muffin cups. Pour the egg mixture over the broccoli and cheese.

Bake in 325°F oven for 15 to 20 minutes. Cool for 10 minutes. Remove from the pans and cool completely. Place in a tightly covered container and freeze for up to 6 weeks.

To serve, place desired number of appetizer-size quiches on a baking sheet. Bake frozen appetizers in a 375°F oven for 20 minutes, or until heated through.

▪ *Broccoli-Cheese Quiche*

■ Pete's-a Pizza

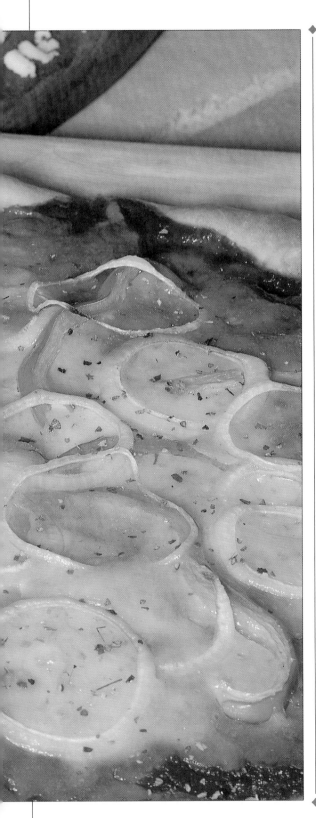

PETE'S-A PIZZA

After a long day of Christmas shopping, you can pull out a frozen homemade pizza, pop it in the oven, and let it bake while you mix up a salad. Or, better yet, stop by a salad bar on your way home.

CRUST:

About 6½ cups bread flour or all-purpose flour, divided
2 packages active dry yeast
2 tablespoons sugar
2 teaspoons salt
2 cups warm (115°F) water
¼ cup cooking or olive oil
About ¼ cup cornmeal

TOPPING OPTIONS:

2 pounds ground beef or bulk pork or Italian sausage, cooked and drained
2 packages (3½ ounces each) sliced pepperoni
2 cans (4 ounces each) sliced ripe olives, drained
½ cup onion, sliced into rings
1 cup (1 large) green pepper, cut into strips
2 cans (4 ounces each) sliced mushrooms, drained

TOPPING MUSTS:

2 cans (15 or 16 ounces each) pizza sauce
4 teaspoons dried oregano, crushed
4 teaspoons dried basil, crushed
2 pounds mozzarella cheese, shredded (8 cups)

TO MAKE THE CRUST: Combine 2½ cups of the flour, the yeast, sugar, and salt in a large bowl. Add the water and oil. With a wooden spoon or electric mixer, beat until smooth. Add the remaining 4 cups flour and mix with a spoon and your hands until blended. (Depending on the humidity, you may need to add ½ cup more flour so the dough is not sticky.)

Knead the dough on a floured surface for 8 to 10 minutes, or until smooth and elastic—the dough will feel as if it is "pushing back." Return the dough to a greased mixing bowl, turning once to grease the surface. Cover and let rise in a warm, draft-free place for 45 minutes, or until doubled in size.

Meanwhile, prepare the optional toppings, if using. The amounts of topping ingredients given are enough for 4 pizzas. You can vary the toppings on each pizza. For example, make 2 with green peppers and onions; 1 with sausage and mushrooms; and 1 with cheese only. Divide the amounts of topping ingredients you need by 4 to get the amount you need for each pizza.

TO PREBAKE THE PIZZA CRUST AND ASSEMBLE PIZZA: Preheat the oven to 425°F. Grease 4 (12-inch) pizza pans, then sprinkle each lightly with cornmeal. Punch down the pizza dough, turn it out, and cut it into 4 equal pieces. Let rest 5 minutes for easier rolling. Roll out each piece of dough into a 13-inch round and place each on a prepared pizza pan, then tuck under the edges of the dough. Prebake the pizza crusts for 12 minutes. Remove the crusts from the pans and place on wire racks.

Spread each pizza evenly with about 1 cup of pizza sauce. Sprinkle with oregano and basil. Add the optional toppings, if using. Sprinkle each pizza with 2 cups of cheese.

TO FREEZE: Carefully wrap each pizza well in vapor- and moisture-proof freezer wrap and seal well. Label and freeze for up to 6 weeks.

TO SERVE: Preheat the oven to 425°F. Unwrap and place a frozen pizza on a greased pizza pan or baking sheet. Bake for 20 minutes, or until the crust is browned and the cheese is melted. Let cool 5 minutes before cutting into wedges.

Makes four 12-inch pizzas (each serves 6)

POTATO GNOCCHI

Gnocchi (pronounced NYO-key) are light dumplings that, when topped with a red pasta sauce and a sprinkle of Parmesan, make a delightful first course before a dinner of fish or poultry. Or, add meat to the pasta sauce and serve as an entrée with Caesar salad and hot, crusty bread. You can also drop the frozen dumplings into simmering vegetable soup minutes before serving time. Although these dumplings are made with potatoes, this recipe is an exception to the general rule that potatoes don't freeze well.

3 pounds potatoes, peeled
2 cups all-purpose flour
4 eggs, lightly beaten
2 teaspoons salt
¼ teaspoon ground nutmeg

TO MAKE: Cube the potatoes and cook them in boiling water, covered, for about 20 minutes, or until tender. Drain and mash. You should have 4 cups. In a large bowl, mix all ingredients. Cover a large baking sheet with waxed paper, plastic wrap, or foil. Fit a pastry bag with a ½-inch-wide tip. Put a quarter of the potato mixture at a time into the bag. Squeeze the bag gently over the baking sheet, squeezing out 1 inch of potato mixture. Turn

the tip down onto the baking sheet to stop the flow and lift the bag to form a dumpling. Continue until all the gnocchi mixture is used and the baking sheet is covered with inch-long dumplings.

TO FREEZE: Place the baking sheet in the freezer for about 2 hours, until the gnocchi are frozen solid. Divide into 2 freezer bags or rigid containers and seal. Label and return to the freezer for up to 6 weeks. (Each bag will contain 4 servings.)

TO SERVE: In a large saucepan or stockpot, bring 5 quarts water to a rolling boil. Add 1 tablespoon salt and 1 teaspoon cooking oil. Pour the contents of 1 container into the water. Return the water to boiling, uncovered, and reduce the heat to a gentle boil. When the gnocchi float to the top, boil 1 minute longer.

Drain in a colander and serve hot, topped with pasta sauce and grated or shredded cheese.

Makes 8 entrée servings

NOTE: If you don't have a pastry bag, you can use a heavy plastic bag instead. Cut ¼ inch off the bottom corner of the bag, then fill the bag no more than half full with gnocchi mixture. Twist the top of the bag down and squeeze mixture out through the hole.

■ *Potato Gnocchi*

■ *Macaroni 'n' Cheese Deluxe*

MACARONI 'N' CHEESE DELUXE

America's favorite meatless casserole, Macaroni 'n' Cheese Deluxe is just the thing after an afternoon of winter skating or shopping. This recipe makes two (2-quart) casseroles. If you want a creamier sauce, substitute half of the Cheddar cheese with 2 cups of American or processed Swiss cheese.

1 pound elbow macaroni
1/2 cup butter or margarine
1/2 cup (1/2 large) chopped red sweet peppers
1/2 cup (1/2 large) chopped green peppers
1/4 cup chopped onions
1/2 cup all-purpose flour
1 1/2 teaspoons dry mustard
5 cups milk
1 pound shredded sharp Cheddar cheese (4 cups)
1 to 2 tablespoons Worcestershire sauce
1/2 teaspoon salt

TO MAKE: Cook the macaroni according to package directions, but only for 6 to 8 minutes, so it is slightly underdone.

Melt the butter or margarine in a large saucepan over medium heat; cook the peppers and onions until tender, but not brown. Stir in the flour and mustard. Stir in the milk and cook, stirring constantly, until thickened and bubbly. Add the cheese, Worcestershire sauce, and salt; stir until the cheese is melted. Gently mix in cooked pasta.

TO FREEZE: Butter two 2-quart oven-proof or microwave-safe casseroles or coat with non-stick spray. (See "Serving Made Easy" on page 72 for wrapping options.) Divide the macaroni and cheese mixture equally between the dishes. Cool for 30 minutes. Wrap the top of the casseroles in plastic wrap and heavy-duty foil and seal. Label and freeze for up to 6 weeks.

TO BAKE: Preheat the oven to 400°F. Remove the plastic wrap from the casserole and cover lightly with the foil. Bake the frozen casserole for 2 hours, or until hot and bubbly, stirring occasionally.

TO MICROWAVE: Remove the foil wrap from microwave-safe casserole and cover with microwave-safe plastic wrap. Heat on 70 percent power for 20 minutes, turning once, until just beginning to thaw. Continue cooking for 15 to 20 minutes longer, stirring every 5 to 10 minutes, until heated through.

Makes two 2-quart casseroles (each serves 6)

SWEDISH MEATBALLS

In Scandinavia, this mixture is formed into flat, oval-shaped patties about 3 inches long and served with fresh cucumber salad or pickled beets, buttered new potatoes, and a hot vegetable. If desired, serve meat with rice, brussels sprouts, and yellow squash. Or, shape meat into bite-size balls, heat in gravy, and serve from a chafing dish.

4 slices white bread, crusts trimmed
1/3 cup milk or water
1 tablespoon butter or margarine
1/4 cup chopped onions
1 pound ground beef
1 pound ground veal
1 pound ground pork
4 eggs
1/4 cup minced fresh parsley

2 teaspoons lemon juice or vinegar
1/4 teaspoon ground nutmeg
1/4 teaspoon salt
1/8 teaspoon ground allspice

TO MAKE: In a small bowl, soak the bread in the milk or water. Meanwhile, melt the butter or margarine in a small skillet and cook the onions until tender. Squeeze the liquid from the bread, and discard the liquid. In a large bowl, mix the bread, onions, beef, veal, pork, eggs, parsley, lemon juice or vinegar, nutmeg, salt, and allspice. Cover and refrigerate for about 1 hour for easier handling.

TO BAKE: Preheat the oven to 375°F. Cover a large baking pan with heavy-duty aluminum foil. Put a wire rack on the foil. (This method of cooking lets the fat drain off.) Form the meat mixture into 1½-inch balls or 3-inch oval-shaped patties and place on the rack. Bake for 15 minutes, or until brown and cooked through. Repeat until all the meatballs are cooked. Drain on paper towels. Loosely wrap and refrigerate the meatballs for about 2 hours, until chilled through.

TO FREEZE: Transfer the meatballs to freezer bags or rigid containers and seal. Label and freeze for up to 3 months.

TO SERVE: In a large skillet, melt 2 tablespoons butter or margarine over medium-low heat. Cook the frozen meatballs in hot butter for about 20 minutes, or until heated through, turning occasionally. Or, heat brown gravy (2 cups for 12 meatballs) in a medium saucepan over medium heat until simmering. Place the frozen meatballs in the gravy and simmer about 15 minutes, or until heated through.

Makes 3 dozen meatballs

ELEGANT STUFFED CHICKEN BREASTS

Save these fancy chicken breasts for special company or when you want to treat your family to a scrumptious meal. Put flowers and candles on the table, and serve the chicken with steamed broccoli, new pototoes, chutney, and hot Parker House rolls.

STUFFING:
6 slices white bread, crusts trimmed
1/4 cup butter or margarine, melted
1 medium Granny Smith apple, peeled, cored, and finely chopped (1 cup)
1 cup fresh or frozen cranberries, chopped
1/4 cup snipped fresh parsley
2 teaspoons sugar
1 teaspoon salt

CHICKEN:
6 whole chicken breasts, halved
About 1/2 cup butter or margarine, divided

TO MAKE THE STUFFING: Cut the bread into 1/2-inch cubes. To toast the bread cubes, bake in a shallow baking pan in a 300°F oven for 15 minutes, stirring twice. In a large bowl, mix together the bread, butter or margarine, apples, cranberries, parsley, sugar, and salt.

TO MAKE THE CHICKEN: Skin the chicken, if desired. Find the natural opening in the side of each chicken breast between the tenderloin and breast meat. (Or, use a sharp knife to make a pocket.) Fill each opening with 1/4 cup stuffing. Refrigerate 6 of the chicken breasts while cooking the rest.

TO COOK: Melt 1/4 cup of the butter or margarine in a 12-inch skillet over medium heat. Brown the remaining 6 chicken breasts bone-side up in the butter for 8 minutes. Turn and reduce the heat to medium-low. Cover tightly and cook for 30 to 35 minutes, or until a meat thermometer registers 170°F in the thickest part of the chicken and 165°F in the stuffing and the meat juices run clear.

TO FREEZE: Remove the chicken and wrap each chicken breast separately in freezer wrap and seal well. Place the wrapped chicken in large bags or boxes. Label and freeze for up to 3 months. Repeat with remaining uncooked chicken, using additional butter or margarine as needed.

TO SERVE: Thaw the cooked chicken, still wrapped, in the refrigerator overnight. (Do not risk food poisoning by thawing chicken at room temperature.) Preheat the oven to 350°F. Unwrap the chicken and place it in a baking dish; cover with foil and bake 25 to 30 minutes, or until heated through and a meat thermometer registers 165°F. You can heat the frozen chicken in a 350°F oven for 1 hour 15 minutes, or until heated through and meat thermometer registers 165°F. Serve with Cider Sauce (see page 85).

Makes 12 servings

▪ *Swedish Meatballs (left)*

CIDER SAUCE: In a small saucepan, combine $1/2$ cup apple cider or juice, $1/2$ cup chicken stock, 1 tablespoon cornstarch, 1 teaspoon brown sugar, and $1/8$ teaspoon dried tarragon, crushed. Cook and stir over medium heat until thickened and bubbly. Cook and stir 2 minutes more. Makes $3/4$ cup (enough for 6 chicken breasts).

STIR-FRY FROZEN MIXTURE

While fresh vegetables are bountiful in your garden or market, freeze some for a quick stir-fry during the holidays. Trim and prepare a total of 1 pound of vegetables (about 4 cups) for stir-frying (choose cauliflower florets, carrot slices, and green beans cut into 1-inch pieces), then blanch them to retard spoilage.

TO STEAM BLANCH: Use a kettle with a tight-fitting lid. Add enough water to come within 1 inch of the bottom of a steamer basket or colander placed in the kettle; bring to boiling. Keep the heat high. Place cauliflower, carrots, and green beans in a single layer in the steamer basket or colander. Cover and steam for 5 minutes. Repeat for remaining vegetables.

TO WATER BLANCH: Place 1 pound of a mixture of cauliflower, carrots, and green beans in a steamer basket. Immerse the vegetables into 1 gallon of boiling water in a large kettle. Cover and boil for 5 minutes.

Quickly cool blanched vegetables by plunging them into ice water for the same amount of time as they were blanched. Drain well. Spread the vegetables onto baking sheets, barely touching. Place in the freezer until frozen solid, then transfer to freezer bags or rigid containers. Label and return to the freezer.

To cook, thaw desired amount of vegetables, then stir-fry in a skillet in 1 to 2 tablespoons hot cooking oil for 3 to 4 minutes, or until crisp and tender. Or, use in a stir-fry with meat or poultry, or cook and stir into heated pasta sauce.

■ *Elegant Stuffed Chicken Breasts*

CHINESE POT STICKERS

Serve these dumplings for a quick family dinner with rice and buttered green beans. They also make wonderful Christmas cocktail party fare, served with tongs from a warm chafing dish or passed to guests on a silver tray. Make a quick dip by mixing half red wine vinegar or rice vinegar and half soy sauce, or by mixing thin apricot jam with a little orange juice. Wonton or pot sticker wrappers are available from Asian grocers and many well-stocked supermarkets.

1 egg, beaten
4 teaspoons soy sauce
2 tablespoons minced green onions
1 tablespoon minced fresh gingerroot
1 clove garlic, minced
1/2 pound ground beef
1/2 pound ground pork
48 (3-inch) wonton or pot sticker wrappers
Cooking oil, for frying

TO MAKE: In a medium bowl, mix together the egg, soy sauce, onions, ginger, and garlic; add the beef and pork. Mix well. Spread a dozen wrappers out on a table. (Keep the remaining wrappers under a damp towel to prevent them from drying out.) Working quickly, put a scant tablespoon of meat filling in the center of each wrapper. Wet the edges of the wrappers and fold over to make a triangle (or a half-circle if using rounds). Press the edges together to seal. Refrigerate completed pot stickers, covered with a slightly damp towel. Repeat until all the wrappers are used.

TO FREEZE: Spread the pot stickers on a baking sheet, barely touching. Cover loosely with foil. Freeze about 2 hours, just until they are frozen through. Transfer the frozen pot stickers to freezer bags or rigid containers and seal. Label and freeze for up to 6 weeks (store in an area of the freezer where they will be protected from breakage).

TO SERVE: Heat 2 tablespoons cooking oil in a 10-inch skillet over medium heat. Carefully (to avoid splattering oil) add just enough frozen pot stickers (about 12) to cover the bottom of the skillet; do not crowd. Cook 1 1/2 to 2 minutes per side, or until brown on both sides. Carefully add 1/4 cup water to skillet; cover tightly and let pot stickers steam over low heat for 8 to 10 minutes, or until cooked through. Cover loosely with foil and keep cooked pot stickers warm in a 300°F oven until serving time. Repeat with remaining frozen pot stickers.

Makes 48

■ *Chinese Pot Stickers*

GARDEN PASTA SAUCE

Here's the ideal way to preserve the last of the ripe tomatoes in your garden and enjoy the convenient, versatile results throughout the holidays. Use this sauce on pasta, gnocchi, or meat loaf, to flavor soups, or in lasagna.

When poured into a pretty jar, this sauce makes a great gift. Give it still frozen and tell the recipient to put it back in the freezer immediately.

½ bushel (about 30 pounds) tomatoes
2 tablespoons cooking or olive oil
1 pound fresh mushrooms, sliced
1 cup chopped onions
1 cup chopped celery
4 cloves garlic, minced
½ cup firmly packed brown sugar
¼ cup chopped fresh parsley
2 tablespoons dried basil, crushed
2 tablespoons dried oregano, crushed
Salt, to taste

TO MAKE: Wash, core, and halve the tomatoes. Place them in an 18-quart heavy enameled or stainless steel pot. Crush some of the tomatoes to release their juice, then bring mixture to a boil, stirring often. Reduce the heat and simmer, uncovered, for 30 minutes, stirring often. Let cool enough to handle. Press through a food mill and discard the seeds and skins. Return strained tomatoes to the pot. (You should have about 11 quarts.)

While the tomatoes are cooking, heat the oil over medium heat in a large skillet. Cook the mushrooms, onions, and celery, covered, for about 8 minutes, or until the onions are beginning to soften; add the garlic and cook, uncovered, for 5 minutes more.

Add the mushroom mixture, sugar, parsley, basil, and oregano to the tomatoes and stir well. Bring to a boil; then reduce the heat and boil gently, uncovered, stirring occasionally, about 4 to 4½ hours, until sauce is reduced and thickened. Stir more often toward the end of the cooking time to prevent sticking. (It may be necessary to reduce heat more as the mixture thickens.) Add salt to taste. Let cool completely, keeping the pot covered. Hasten cooling by placing the pot in a sinkful of ice water.

TO FREEZE: Pour cooled sauce into quart-size self-sealing freezer bags or freezer containers, leaving a 1-inch headspace; seal. Label and freeze for up to 6 months. If using bags, place them flat on a baking sheet in 1 layer.

TO SERVE: Defrost the sauce partially to remove it from the container, then heat it in a pan on the stovetop. Or, place the sauce in a microwave-safe container and defrost and heat in a microwave oven according to the manufacturer's directions.

Makes 4 quarts

▪ *Garden Pasta Sauce*

CHAPTER 2

Yeast Breads and Quick Breads

FEW EXPERIENCES CAN GIVE YOU THE CONTENT FEELING YOU GET FROM MAKING BREAD—THE FEELING YOU GET FROM THE WARM, HOMEY AROMA OF THE YEAST, THE SILKY COOLNESS OF FLOUR, THE SATISFACTION OF FEELING THE DOUGH RESPOND AS YOU KNEAD IT, AND THEN SEEING IT RISE TO A GOLDEN LOAF OF HOMEMADE BREAD.

THE FOLLOWING RECIPES GIVE YOU ALL THE INITIAL CONTENT-

MENT OF BAKING BREAD PLUS INSTANT GRATIFICATION WHEN YOU PULL A LOAF OR A BATCH OF ROLLS FROM YOUR FREEZER. BE SURE TO READ "SUCCESSFUL FREEZING" ON PAGE 72 FOR HINTS ABOUT WRAPPING AND FREEZING YOUR HOMEMADE BREADS AND ROLLS. BREAD THAT IS FROZEN AS SOON AS IT COOLS RETAINS ALL ITS FLAVOR AND TEXTURE WHEN IT'S DEFROSTED OR HEATED.

BREADMAKING BASICS

If you haven't made bread before, you'll be surprised at how easy it can be. Just follow the instructions in any of these recipes exactly and success is guaranteed. Remember that the yeast does most of the work—in its own good time. Most of the time involved in breadmaking is spent in waiting for the yeast to grow.

Kneading is an essential step; it gives the dough a structure that will hold the gases created by the growing yeast. Get in there and enjoy kneading the dough. It's a great way to relieve stress!

Quick breads are wonderful in a different way. Faster to make than yeast breads, they are generally more moist, and have a more "cake-like" texture. Like yeast breads, quick breads freeze beautifully, so go ahead and make several loaves to have on hand for holiday guests and gift-giving. Save an extra loaf or two to surprise your favorite football fans on Super Bowl Sunday in January.

WHOLE-WHEAT DINNER ROLLS

These no-knead refrigerator rolls do double duty. You can keep a batch of dough in the refrigerator for up to two days to form into rolls and bake before dinner. Or, you can go ahead and partially bake the rolls, then freeze them to brown and serve as they are needed.

3 cups all-purpose flour, divided
2 packages active dry yeast
1½ cups water
¼ cup sugar
¼ cup butter or margarine
2 teaspoons salt
1 egg, lightly beaten
2 cups whole-wheat flour

TO MAKE: Combine 2 cups of the all-purpose flour and yeast in a large bowl. In a saucepan, heat and stir the water, sugar, butter or margarine, and salt until warm (120° to 130°F) and the butter or margarine almost melts. Add to the flour mixture along with the egg. Beat with an electric mixer at low speed until combined. Beat at high speed for 3 minutes. Stir in the whole-wheat flour and the remaining all-purpose flour until the dough is soft and just slightly sticky. Cover the bowl with plastic wrap and refrigerate for at least 2 hours and up to 48 hours. (The time in the refrigerator is necessary for letting the dough rest and develop flavor.)

To form cloverleaf rolls, first lightly grease muffin cups, or coat with nonstick spray. Remove the bread dough from the refrigerator and punch the dough to release air bubbles. Break off pieces of dough, roll them into 1-inch balls, placing 3 pieces in each muffin cup. If desired, lightly brush the tops of the rolls with cooking oil or melted butter or margarine.

Cover the rolls lightly with plastic wrap and leave in a warm place to rise for 1 hour, or until double in bulk. For brown-and-serve rolls, bake in a 325°F oven for 15 minutes and remove them from the oven before they start to brown. Turn rolls out onto wire racks and cool completely before freezing. If desired, bake the rolls without freezing by shaping them, then letting them rise for 1 hour, or until double in bulk. Bake in a 375°F oven for 12 to 15 minutes, or until golden brown.

TO FREEZE: Place the rolls on a baking sheet and freeze about 1 to 2 hours, until solid. Remove the rolls from the freezer and transfer to freezer bags or freezer containers, or use freezer wrap, and seal. Label and return to the freezer for up to 3 months.

TO SERVE: Preheat the oven to 350°F. Place the frozen rolls on a baking sheet or in muffin cups and bake 12 to 15 minutes, or until golden brown.

Makes about 3 dozen rolls

VARIATIONS: Form the rolls into any shape you like. For simple round rolls, break off golf-ball-size pieces of dough and place them, just barely touching each other, in a lightly greased square or rectangular baking pan.

▪ *Whole-Wheat Dinner Rolls*

SWEDISH CARLQUIST CARDAMOM BREAD

My friend, Bethany Brinton, who lives in Winston-Salem, North Carolina, gave me the recipe for this wonderful braided bread that is a Christmas tradition in her Swedish family.

1 cup warm (115°F) water
1 package active dry yeast
½ cup nonfat dry milk powder
4½ to 5 cups all-purpose flour, divided
2 eggs
½ cup sugar
6 tablespoons butter or margarine, softened
1 teaspoon salt
1 teaspoon ground cardamom or the seeds from 6 whole cardamom pods, crushed
Milk, for brushing

TO MAKE: Pour the water into a medium bowl; add the yeast, dry milk, and 1 cup of the flour. Let rest for 10 minutes, or until slightly bubbly. Beat in the eggs, sugar, butter or margarine, salt, and cardamom. One cup at a time, add as much of the remaining flour as you can, beating well with a wooden spoon until the dough is thick and soft.

Turn the dough out onto a floured board and knead in enough of the remaining flour to make a moderately soft dough that is smooth and elastic (about 3 to 5 minutes). Place in a lightly greased bowl; turn once to grease surface. Cover and set in a warm place about 1½ hours, or until doubled in bulk.

With your fist, punch the dough to release air bubbles. Turn it out onto a lightly floured board and cut in half. Let rest for 10 minutes. Lightly grease a very large baking sheet, or coat with nonstick spray.

Cut each half into 3 equal pieces. Roll each piece of dough between your palms and a lightly floured board to make ropes about 1" in diameter and 14" long. Using 3 ropes, make a loose braid. Pinch the ends together to seal, then turn the ends under about 2 inches and pinch to seal. Place on a baking sheet. Repeat with the other 3 ropes. Cover loosely with plastic wrap and leave in a warm place to rise for about 45 minutes to 1 hour, until double in bulk. Brush gently with milk. About 15 minutes before the end of the rising period, preheat the oven to 350°F. Bake for 25 to 30 minutes, or until light brown and the loaf sounds hollow when the crust is tapped. Transfer to wire racks and cool completely.

TO FREEZE: Place the loaves on a baking sheet and freeze for about 3 hours, until frozen solid. Transfer to freezer bags or freezer wrap and seal. Label and return to the freezer for up to 3 months.

TO SERVE: Defrost, still wrapped, at room temperature for at least 2 hours; or unwrap and defrost in a microwave oven according to the manufacturer's directions. If desired, tear, rather than cut, servings from the loaves to get the full texture and aroma of the bread.

Makes 2 braided loaves (each loaf serves 8)

▪ *Swedish Carlquist Cardamom Bread*

PANNETONE

An Italian Christmas bread, Pannetone has a light yet moist texture and is served for breakfast, with afternoon coffee, or on a dessert buffet. Keep a loaf or two to serve drop-in guests and include a loaf in an Italian-theme gift basket.

SPONGE:

1 cup warm (115°F) water
2 packages active dry yeast
1 teaspoon sugar
1 cup all-purpose flour

DOUGH:

1 cup hot (140°F) water
1 cup nonfat dry milk powder
1 cup sugar
1/2 cup butter or margarine
1 tablespoon grated orange peel (no white)
2 teaspoons salt
1 teaspoon vanilla
5 egg yolks, lightly beaten
7 to 8 cups all-purpose flour, divided
1 cup golden raisins plumped in 1 cup warm
    water or apple juice, then drained well
1/2 cup chopped candied citron
1/2 cup chopped candied orange peel
Fine dry bread crumbs or matzo meal
1 egg mixed with 1 tablespoon water, for glazing

TO MAKE THE SPONGE: In a medium bowl, stir together the sponge ingredients. Let rest for 10 minutes, or until bubbly and the surface looks like a sponge.

TO MAKE THE DOUGH: In a large bowl, mix together the hot water, dry milk, sugar, butter or margarine, grated orange peel, salt, and vanilla, stirring to melt the butter. Add the "sponge," egg yolks, 2 cups of the flour, raisins, citron, and candied orange peel; mix well.

Add additional flour, 1 cup at a time, stirring well after each addition, until the dough makes a ball and is just slightly sticky.

Turn the dough out onto a floured board and knead about 8 to 10 minutes, until smooth and elastic. The dough will be fairly soft. Place the dough in a greased bowl; turn once to grease surface. Cover and set in a warm place about 1 1/2 hours, until doubled in bulk.

Punch the dough to release air bubbles. Turn dough out onto a lightly floured surface and cut into 4 equal pieces. Let rest for 10 minutes.

Grease four 8" x 4" loaf pans or 3 or 4 cup soufflé dishes and sprinkle lightly with bread crumbs or matzo meal; tap out the excess. Form each piece of dough into a loaf or ball and place into prepared pans. Or, shape into 4 round loaves and place on greased baking sheets. Cover and let dough rise in a warm place about 1 hour, until nearly double in size. (The bread will rise further in the oven.)

Preheat the oven to 350°F. Glaze the tops of the loaves with the egg/water mixture. Bake for 35 to 45 minutes, or until golden brown. Turn out onto wire racks and cool completely.

TO FREEZE: Place the cooled loaves in freezer bags or use freezer wrap and seal. Label and freeze for up to 3 months.

TO SERVE: Defrost, still wrapped, at room temperature for 2 hours, or unwrap and defrost in a microwave oven according to the manufacturer's directions.

If you like, sprinkle well with powdered sugar. Or, drizzle with a glaze made of 1 cup powdered sugar, 1 teaspoon vanilla, and enough milk to make a glaze consistency; then decorate with candied red and green cherry halves and small silver decorative balls (see page 119).

Makes 4 loaves

Pannetone

DANISH COFFEECAKE

This fruit-filled coffeecake, with its rich, buttery, flaky texture, is delicious served warm or at room temperature. Your family and guests are sure to say "Wow!"

DOUGH:

1 cup butter

2 tablespoons all-purpose flour

5 to 5½ cups all-purpose flour, divided

2 packages active dry yeast

½ cup nonfat dry milk powder

1¼ cups water

½ cup sugar

¼ cup butter or margarine

1 teaspoon salt

2 eggs, lightly beaten

FILLING:

2 cups finely chopped dried apricots, prunes, figs, or dates

½ cup water

½ cup sugar

¼ cup lemon juice

2 tablespoons butter or margarine

1 egg yolk mixed with 1 tablespoon water, for glazing

TO MAKE THE DOUGH: In a medium mixing bowl, combine the 1 cup butter and 2 tablespoons flour. Roll the mixture between 2 large sheets of waxed paper into a 10"x 6" rectangle. Chill for 1 hour in the refrigerator.

In a large mixing bowl, combine 1½ cups of the flour, yeast, and dry milk. In a saucepan, heat and stir the water, sugar, ¼ cup butter or margarine, and salt until warm (120° to 130°F) and the butter almost melts. Add to the flour mixture along with the eggs. Beat with an electric mixer for 3 minutes at high speed. Stir in as much of the remaining flour as you can with a spoon. On a lightly floured surface, knead in enough remaining flour to make a moderately soft dough that is smooth and elastic (3 to 5 minutes). Cover and let rest 10 minutes.

On a floured surface, roll the dough into a 12"x 10" rectangle. Remove 1 sheet of waxed paper from the chilled butter rectangle. Invert it onto one end of the dough; remove the second sheet of waxed paper. Fold the other side of the dough over the butter, pressing the edges to seal them. With a floured rolling pin, roll the folded dough to a 12"x 16" rectangle. Fold the dough crosswise into thirds to form a 12"x 5" rectangle. Cover and chill for 1 hour. Roll and fold twice more, ending with a 12"x 5" folded piece of dough. Cover and chill dough for several hours or overnight.

TO MAKE THE FILLING: In a small saucepan, stir together the fruit, water, sugar, and lemon juice. (If using apricots, omit lemon juice and add ¼ cup more water.) Heat, stirring constantly, until thickened. Stir in the butter or margarine. Cover and chill until needed.

TO BAKE: Lightly grease 2 baking sheets, or coat them with nonstick spray. Cut the dough rectangle in half crosswise. Refrigerate one half until needed. On a lightly floured surface, roll one half of the dough to a 12"x 18" rectangle. Spread with half the chilled filling, leaving 1 inch on all sides. Starting from a long side, roll dough jelly-roll style. Pinch the seam to seal. Transfer to a baking sheet, seam side down. Bring the ends together to form a ring; brush the ends with water and pinch together to seal. With kitchen shears or a sharp knife, snip about ½ inch into the top of the ring at 2-inch intervals. These slits will open during rising and baking, revealing part of the filling.

Danish Coffeecake

Repeat with the remaining half of the dough and filling.

Cover the dough rings loosely with plastic wrap and let rise in a warm place until nearly doubled in bulk (about 1 hour). Brush lightly with the egg/water mixture (this will give the rings a shiny, golden finish). Bake in a 375°F oven for 25 to 30 minutes, or until the bread is done, covering with foil the last 10 minutes to prevent over-browning. Transfer to wire racks and cool completely.

TO FREEZE: Place the rings on baking sheets and freeze about 4 hours, until solid. Transfer to freezer bags or use freezer wrap and seal. Label and return to the freezer for up to 3 months.

TO SERVE: Thaw, still wrapped, at room temperature for 1 hour, or remove wrap and thaw and warm in a microwave oven according to the manufacturer's directions. If desired, drizzle with powdered sugar icing.

Makes 2 coffeecakes (each serves 8)

FRENCH BREAD MIX

Here's a bread dough mix designed to stir up the dry ingredients now; simply add warm water when you're ready to make bread. This dough also makes great pizza crust and bread sticks. Invite the children to form the dough into initials, turtles, snakes, or balls. For small rolls and shapes, the rising and baking times will be shorter than indicated in the recipe. Serve the bread the same day you bake it.

For a nice gift, pour the mix into a pretty canister, include baking directions, and put them in a gift basket with a bread board, a jar of homemade jam, and a pot of honey.

6 cups bread flour
1 tablespoon sugar
1 package active dry yeast
2 teaspoons salt

TO MAKE THE MIX: In a large bowl, mix all ingredients together. Transfer to a glass or plastic container. Store in the refrigerator or freezer. Check the package of yeast for its expiration date; the mix will be usable until that date.

TO MAKE THE BREAD: Transfer the dry bread mix to a very large bowl. Make a well in the center and add 2 cups very warm water (120° to 130°F). Stir gradually with a wooden spoon, mixing in dry ingredients from the sides. The dough will get thick and heavy. Continue stirring until all the flour is incorporated. Depending on humidity, you may need to add additional flour so that the dough will be just barely sticky.

Turn the dough out onto a floured board and knead (adding more flour, if necessary, to make a stiff dough) for 8 to 10 minutes.

Return the dough to the bowl, cover with plastic wrap, and let rise in a warm place for about 1 hour, until doubled in bulk.

Grease 2 baking sheets. Punch the dough to release air bubbles. Cut the dough into 2 pieces. Roll 1 piece to a rectangle 10"x 12" on a lightly floured surface. Shape into a loaf by starting at the short end and rolling up, jelly-roll style. Pinch the seam to seal, then turn under each end of the roll to form a neat loaf about 10 inches long. Place on a baking sheet, tapering the ends. Repeat with the remaining half of dough.

Cover the loaves loosely with plastic wrap and leave in a warm place to rise for about 45 minutes, until double in bulk. The bread will rise further during baking. About 15 minutes before the end of the rising time, preheat the oven to 375°F. If you want a crunchy, light-colored crust, brush or spray the tops with water. For a dark, shiny crust, mix 1 egg with 1 tablespoon water and brush on top of the loaves. Slash the tops diagonally 3 or 4 times. Bake for 25 to 30 minutes, or until the bread sounds hollow when you tap the crust. Turn out onto wire racks and let cool before slicing.

Makes 2 loaves

■ *French Bread Mix*

SWEET HARVEST QUICK BREAD

If you've tasted zucchini bread, you already know the moistness and flavor a vegetable can add to a quick bread. These big, luscious, sweet loaves incorporate finely shredded apples with some favorite fall vegetables. The loaves keep very well in the refrigerator for two weeks or in the freezer for three months.

2 cups all-purpose flour
1 cup whole-wheat flour
1 cup sugar
1 cup firmly packed brown sugar
2 teaspoons baking soda
1 teaspoon salt
1 teaspoon ground cinnamon
1 teaspoon ground allspice
4 eggs, lightly beaten
1 cup cooking oil
$3/4$ cup tomato juice or orange juice
$1/2$ cup finely shredded carrots
$1/2$ cup finely shredded unpeeled zucchini
$1/2$ cup finely shredded unpeeled yellow
    summer squash
$1/2$ cup peeled, cored, and finely shredded
    apple

■ *Sweet Harvest Quick Bread*

TO MAKE: Preheat the oven to 350°F and grease two 9"x 5"x 3" loaf pans.

In a large bowl, stir together the all-purpose flour, whole-wheat flour, sugar, brown sugar, baking soda, salt, cinnamon, and allspice until well combined. Form a well in the center. In a medium bowl, combine the eggs, oil, tomato or orange juice, carrots, zucchini, yellow squash, and apples. Add to the flour mixture, stirring just until combined; do not overmix. Divide the batter evenly between the prepared loaf pans. Bake for 45 to 55 minutes, or until a toothpick inserted near the center comes out clean. Remove the bread from the oven and cool on wire racks for 15 minutes. Remove from pans and cool on the racks completely.

If you are not freezing the loaves, wrap them well in plastic wrap. Let stand at room temperature for 24 hours before slicing. Store at room temperature for up to 2 days or in the refrigerator for up to 2 weeks.

TO FREEZE: Wrap well in freezer wrap or freezer bags and seal. Label and freeze for up to 3 months.

TO SERVE: Unwrap and defrost at room temperature. Or, unwrap and defrost in a microwave oven according to the manufacturer's directions. Cut into 1-inch slices.

Makes 2 loaves

VARIATION: You can vary the amounts of grated apples and vegetables, using any or all of them, as long as there is a total of 2 cups.

LEMON-POPPY SEED QUICK BREAD

The perky lemon flavor with the mild crunch of poppy seeds makes these loaves irresistible. The texture is much like pound cake, so you can slice them thinly, spread the slices with cream cheese (if desired), and serve as tea sandwiches. You have the option to bake the batter in a tube pan or in a loaf pan.

BREAD:
$2/3$ cup butter or margarine
2 cups sugar
2 teaspoons finely shredded lemon peel
4 eggs
3 cups all-purpose flour
$1/3$ cup poppy seeds
2 teaspoons baking powder
1 teaspoon salt
$1 1/4$ cups milk
$1/4$ cup lemon juice

TOPPING:
1 cup sifted powdered sugar
$1/2$ cup lemon juice

TO MAKE THE BREAD: Preheat the oven to 350°F. Grease and flour two 8"x 4"x 2" loaf pans or one 10-inch plain or fluted tube pan.

In a large bowl, cream the butter or margarine, sugar, and lemon peel until fluffy. Add the eggs, 1 at a time, beating well after each addition. In a medium bowl, stir together the flour, poppy seeds, baking powder, and salt. Add the flour mixture, one-third at a time, alternately with the milk to the butter/sugar mixture, beginning and ending with the flour mixture. Stir in the lemon juice.

Divide the batter evenly between the prepared loaf pans or pour into the tube pan. Bake about 1 hour, or until a toothpick inserted near the center comes out clean.

TO MAKE THE TOPPING: While the bread is baking, heat the powdered sugar and lemon juice in a small saucepan just until hot, stirring constantly.

Remove the bread from the oven. Cool on wire racks for 15 minutes. Remove from pan(s). Immediately poke each loaf 12 times or the bread in the tube pan 25 times, using a meat fork. Place the bread on wire racks over waxed paper. Spoon the topping over the hot bread. Cool completely.

If you are not freezing the loaves or cake, wrap them well in plastic wrap. Let them rest for 24 hours before slicing. Store at room temperature for up to 2 days or in the refrigerator for up to 2 weeks.

TO FREEZE: Wrap well in plastic freezer wrap or freezer bags and seal. Label and freeze for up to 3 months.

TO SERVE: Unwrap and defrost at room temperature. Or, unwrap and defrost in microwave oven according to the manufacturer's directions. Slice.

Makes 2 loaves or 1 tube

VARIATION: Make Orange-Poppy Seed Quick Bread by substituting orange juice for the lemon juice and 1 tablespoon orange peel for the lemon peel.

■ *Lemon-Poppy Seed Quick Bread (left); Prune Quick Bread (right)*

PRUNE QUICK BREAD

For as long as I can remember, this incredibly moist, spicy bread has been birthday "cake" for my brother, Brent Franklin, who lives in New Orleans. Much lower in fat than many fruit breads, it's sure to be a year-round favorite at your house, too.

2 cups coarsely chopped pitted prunes
2 cups boiling water

1 cup sugar
2 eggs
¼ cup butter or margarine, melted
1 teaspoon vanilla
4 cups all-purpose flour
1 tablespoon baking powder
1 tablespoon ground cinnamon
¾ teaspoon salt
½ teaspoon ground nutmeg
**1 cup coarsely chopped walnuts
   (optional)**

TO MAKE: Preheat the oven to 350°F. Grease two 8"x 4"x 2" loaf pans.

In a medium bowl, cover the prunes with the water; cool to lukewarm (about 20 minutes). Drain the prunes, reserving the liquid. In a large bowl, beat the sugar, eggs, butter or margarine, and vanilla until well blended. In another large bowl, stir the flour, baking powder, cinnamon, salt, and nutmeg together. Add to the sugar mixture, about one-third at a time, alternately with the reserved prune liquid, beginning and ending with the flour mixture. Beat with an electric mixer at low speed just until smooth. (The batter may be thick.) With a wooden spoon, gently stir in the prunes and walnuts, if using.

Evenly divide into the prepared loaf pans and bake for about 50 minutes, or until the loaves begin to pull away from the sides of the pans and a toothpick inserted near the center comes out clean. Remove from the oven and cool on wire racks for 15 minutes. Remove from pans and cool completely.

If you are not freezing the loaves, wrap them well in plastic wrap. Store them at room temperature for 24 hours before slicing. Store at room temperature for up to 2 days or in the refrigerator for up to 2 weeks.

TO FREEZE: Wrap well in freezer wrap or freezer bags and seal. Label and freeze for up to 3 months.

TO SERVE: Unwrap and defrost at room temperature for about 3 hours. Or, unwrap and defrost in a microwave oven on 30 percent power for 3 to 5 minutes. Cut into ½-inch slices.

Makes 2 loaves

VARIATIONS: Add pecans instead of walnuts. Make Apricot Quick Bread by omitting cinnamon and substituting dried apricots for the prunes.

CHEDDAR CHEESE AND ONION QUICK BREAD

Serve slices of this flavorful savory bread on a buffet table next to ham or turkey. If there's any left over, use it as a base for hot turkey sandwiches topped with giblet gravy.

4 cups all-purpose flour
2 tablespoons baking powder
1 teaspoon baking soda
1 teaspoon salt
½ pound shredded sharp Cheddar cheese (2 cups)
1 cup chopped onions
1 tablespoon caraway seeds (optional)
4 eggs
2 cups dairy sour cream or plain yogurt

TO MAKE: Preheat the oven to 350°F. Grease two 9"x 5"x 3" or 8"x 4"x 2" loaf pans.

In a large bowl, stir together the flour, baking powder, baking soda, and salt. Stir in the cheese, onions, and caraway seeds, if using. Make a well in the center of the mixture. In a small bowl, stir together the eggs and sour cream or yogurt. Pour the egg mixture into the well in the dry ingredients and stir just until combined. Do not overmix. Evenly divide into the prepared loaf pans and bake for 45 minutes, or until the loaves begin to pull away from the sides of the pans and a toothpick inserted near the center comes out clean. Remove from the oven and cool on wire racks

for 10 minutes. Remove from the pans and cool completely.

If you are not freezing the loaves, wrap them well in plastic wrap. Store at room temperature for 24 hours before slicing. Store in the refrigerator for up to 1 week.

TO FREEZE: Wrap well in freezer wrap, heavy-duty aluminum foil, or freezer bags and seal. Label and freeze for up to 3 months.

TO SERVE: Unwrap and defrost at room temperature. Or, unwrap and defrost in a microwave oven according to the manufacturer's directions. Cut into thin slices.

To reheat conventionally, bake frozen, foil-wrapped bread in a 375°F oven for 25 minutes, or until heated through.

Makes 2 loaves

■ *Cheddar Cheese and Onion Quick Bread*

Make-Ahead Desserts

START NOW TO MAKE YOUR FREEZ-
ER A BAKE SHOP FULL OF HOME-
MADE HOLIDAY GOODIES READY TO
SERVE IN AN INSTANT. WHETHER
YOU'RE PLANNING A DESSERT
BUFFET TO SERVE CHRISTMAS
CAROLERS OR YOU WANT JUST ONE
IMPRESSIVE DESSERT TO TOP OFF A
WONDERFUL DINNER, YOU CAN PRE-
PARE THE COMPONENTS NOW, WRAP
THEM WELL FOR FREEZING, THEN

DECORATE AND GARNISH JUST
BEFORE SERVING.

IN THIS SECTION, YOU'LL FIND
RECIPES FOR SOME GORGEOUS TRA-
DITIONAL AND NEW DESSERTS AS
WELL AS SOME BASICS, INCLUDING
A FLAKY PIE CRUST AND LIGHT,
GOLDEN CREAM PUFF SHELLS TO
MAKE NOW AND FILL LATER.

BEFORE BEGINNING ANY RECIPE
IN THIS CHAPTER, READ "SUCCESSFUL
FREEZING" ON PAGE 72.

Cakes

CHRISTMAS-IN-WILLIAMSBURG FRUITCAKE

This fruitcake is simply the best! Candied cranberries and dried apricots give a very pleasant tartness to this rich, mildly spiced cake. True, it takes time to make, but you'll love the results.

Start making the Candied Cranberries about a week before you plan to make the cake. Like most fruitcakes, this cake needs to age for at least two weeks before slicing.

CANDIED CRANBERRIES:

2½ cups sugar

1½ cups water

4 cups fresh cranberries, washed and drained

CAKE:

2 cups Candied Cranberries, chopped

1½ cups dried apricots, chopped

1½ cups golden raisins

½ cup diced candied citron

2 cups pecans, coarsely chopped

1 cup walnuts, coarsely chopped

½ cup orange marmalade

½ teaspoon vanilla

½ teaspoon almond extract

4 cups all-purpose flour

½ teaspoon baking powder

½ teaspoon salt

1 teaspoon ground cinnamon

½ teaspoon ground mace

½ teaspoon ground cloves

½ teaspoon ground allspice

¼ teaspoon ground nutmeg

1 cup butter

2¼ cups sugar

6 eggs

TO MAKE THE CANDIED CRANBERRIES: In a large saucepan, stir the sugar and water until the sugar is dissolved, then bring to a boil over high heat. Put the cranberries in a stainless steel or heat-proof glass mixing bowl. Pour the boiling syrup over the cranberries. Pour 2 inches of water into a very large saucepan or kettle. Place the bowl of cranberries in the kettle, cover tightly, and steam over low heat for 45 minutes. Remove the bowl from the kettle and let cool, without stirring, for about 1 hour.

Cover the bowl very loosely and place in the refrigerator for 3 to 4 days, stirring occasionally. Remove the cranberries from the syrup and place on sheets of waxed paper for 4 to 5 days to dry at room temperature. Turn the cranberries occasionally for uniform drying.

Store in a covered container in the refrigerator for up to 1 month. Cranberries not used in the cake can be served as candy or can stud a baked ham.

TO MAKE THE CAKE: The day before baking, in a large bowl, mix the cranberries, apricots, raisins, citron, pecans, walnuts, marmalade, vanilla, and almond extract. Cover and leave at room temperature overnight.

Preheat the oven to 300°F. Grease a 10-inch tube pan.

In a large bowl, stir together the flour, baking powder, salt, cinnamon, mace, cloves, allspice, and nutmeg; set aside.

In another large bowl, cream the butter until light, then gradually beat in the sugar until fluffy. Add the eggs, 1 at a time, beating well after each addition. Add the flour mixture 1 cup at a time, beating just until mixed. Stir in the fruit mixture.

Spoon the batter into the prepared pan. Put a pan of water on the bottom rack of the oven. Bake the cake on the center rack for about 2½ hours, or until the edges of the cake begin to pull away from the sides of the pan and a wooden skewer inserted near the center comes out clean. Cover the cake loosely with foil after 1 hour of baking to prevent over-browning.

Cool the cake in the pan for 30 minutes, then turn out onto a wire rack. Turn cake right side up and let cool.

TO AGE: Dampen cheesecloth with rum, brandy, or fruit juice and wrap it around the cake. Wrap well in foil, then place in an air-tight container. Store in the refrigerator for at least 2 weeks and up to 2 months, to mellow flavors. Remoisten the cheesecloth with rum, brandy, or juice about once a week, or as needed.

TO FREEZE: Seal aged fruitcake in freezer containers. Label and freeze for up to 6 months.

TO SERVE: Thaw, loosely covered, for about 4 hours.

Makes one 10-inch tube

■ *Christmas-in-Williamsburg Fruitcake*

CINNAMON-CHOCOLATE COFFEECAKE

This moist, tasty cake freezes beautifully and is delicious served for brunch, afternoon tea, or as dessert. A slice with a glass of milk before bed is a tempting idea, too.

TOPPING:

1 cup coarsely chopped pecans or walnuts
1 cup miniature semisweet chocolate pieces
1/2 cup firmly packed light brown sugar
1 1/2 teaspoons ground cinnamon

CAKE:

3/4 cup butter or margarine, softened
1 cup sugar
1/2 cup firmly packed light brown sugar
2 teaspoons vanilla
3 eggs
3 cups all-purpose flour
1 tablespoon baking powder
1 teaspoon baking soda
1 teaspoon salt
1 1/2 cups plain yogurt

TO MAKE THE TOPPING: In a small bowl, mix together all the topping ingredients. Set aside.

TO MAKE THE CAKE: Preheat the oven to 350°F. Grease and flour a 10-inch fluted or plain tube pan.

In a large bowl, cream together the butter or margarine, sugar, brown sugar, and vanilla, scraping the bowl frequently, until the mixture is light and fluffy. Add the eggs, 1 at a time, beating well after each addition.

In a medium bowl, stir together the flour, baking powder, baking soda, and salt. Add the flour mixture alternately with the yogurt to the butter/sugar mixture, adding the dry ingre-dients in 3 parts and the yogurt in 2 parts. (The batter will be thick.)

Spread one-third of the batter in the prepared pan. Sprinkle with half the topping mixture. Carefully spread the remaining batter over topping, then sprinkle with the remaining topping. Bake for 50 to 60 minutes, or until a toothpick inserted in the center comes out clean.

Cool on a wire rack for 15 minutes, then remove from the pan and cool thoroughly.

TO FREEZE: Wrap well in freezer wrap and seal. Label and freeze for up to 3 months. Place in a box to protect it, if you like.

TO SERVE: Unwrap and defrost for 3 hours, or defrost and reheat in a microwave oven on 30 percent power, uncovered, on a microwave-safe plate for 12 to 15 minutes or until just warm, giving the cake a quarter turn every 5 minutes.

Makes 1 cake (serves 16)

▪ *Cinnamon-Chocolate Coffeecake*

▪ *Aunt Snookum's Chocolate Pound Cake*

AUNT SNOOKUM'S CHOCOLATE POUND CAKE

1 cup butter or margarine, softened
1/2 cup shortening
1 3/4 cups sugar
5 eggs
2 1/2 cups all-purpose flour
1/3 cup unsweetened cocoa powder
1 1/2 teaspoons baking powder
1/2 teaspoon salt
1/4 teaspoon baking soda
1 cup milk
2 teaspoons vanilla

TO MAKE: Preheat the oven to 325°F. Grease and flour a 10-inch fluted or plain tube pan or two 9" x 5" x 3" or 8" x 4" x 2" loaf pans.

In a large mixer bowl, cream the butter or margarine and shortening. Add the sugar gradually, and beat until fluffy—about 5 minutes—scraping the sides of the bowl frequently. Add the eggs, 1 at a time, beating well after each addition.

In a medium bowl, sift together the flour, cocoa powder, baking powder, salt, and baking soda. Set aside. Mix the milk and vanilla in a small bowl, and add alternately with the flour mixture to the butter/sugar mixture, adding the flour mixture in 4 parts and the milk in 3 parts. Mix thoroughly. (The batter may look curdled.) Pour the batter into the prepared pan. Bake tube pan for 75 minutes or loaf pans for 65 to 75 minutes, or until a toothpick inserted in the center comes out clean. Cool on a wire rack for 15 minutes, then turn out of the pan and cool completely.

TO FREEZE: Wrap well in freezer wrap and seal. Label and freeze for up to 6 months. Place in a box to protect it, if you like.

TO SERVE: Unwrap and defrost for 3 hours. Sprinkle with powdered sugar. If desired, serve with whipped cream or ice cream, or drizzle with warm fudge sauce before slicing.

Makes 1 large cake (serves 16)

PUMPKIN NUT ROLL

This dessert is a fancy version of pumpkin cake with cream cheese frosting. Here, a light, spicy sponge cake is rolled around a luscious cream cheese filling and served in slices so the swirls show nicely.

CAKE:
Powdered sugar
3 eggs
1 cup sugar
2/3 cup canned pumpkin
1 teaspoon lemon juice
3/4 cup all-purpose flour
1 tablespoon pumpkin pie spice
1 teaspoon baking powder
1/4 teaspoon salt
1 cup walnuts or pecans, finely chopped

FILLING:
1 package (8 ounces) cream cheese, softened
1/4 cup butter or margarine, softened
1/2 teaspoon vanilla
1 1/4 cups sifted powdered sugar
1 tablespoon finely chopped crystallized ginger

TO MAKE: Preheat the oven to 375°F. Grease and flour a 10" x 15" x 1" jelly-roll pan. Sprinkle a clean dish towel liberally with powdered sugar and set aside.

In a large bowl, beat the eggs with an electric mixer on high speed for 5 minutes.

Gradually add the sugar and continue beating until light and fluffy. Stir in the pumpkin and lemon juice.

In a small bowl, stir together the flour, pumpkin pie spice, baking powder, and salt. Gently fold the dry ingredients into the pumpkin mixture.

Spread the batter evenly in the prepared pan. Sprinkle with the nuts. Bake for 15 minutes, or until the cake springs back when lightly touched.

While still hot, turn the cake out onto the sugar-covered towel and cut off any crispy edges with a sharp knife. Roll up the cake with the towel from the short end and place on a wire rack to cool.

TO MAKE THE FILLING: While the cake cools, beat together the cream cheese, butter or margarine, and vanilla in a medium bowl. Add the sifted powdered sugar gradually, beating until smooth. Stir in the ginger.

Unroll the cooled cake and spread evenly with filling, then roll it up again (without the towel).

TO FREEZE: Put the pumpkin roll on a baking sheet and place it in the freezer for about 6 hours, until frozen solid. Wrap well with freezer wrap or place in a freezer bag and seal. Label and return to the freezer for up to 4 months. Place in a box to protect it, if you like.

TO SERVE: Unwrap and thaw at room temperature for 2 hours. (Do not thaw in a microwave oven oven.) Sprinkle with additional powdered sugar, cut into 1-inch slices, and serve cold. Refrigerate any leftovers.

Makes 1 cake roll (serves 10)

■ *Pumpkin Nut Roll*

CASSATA A LA LITTLE ITALY

Here's a spectacular variation on a classic Italian dessert. Put the cake and filling together and make the frosting to freeze now; then at serving time, you only have to frost and decorate the dessert.

CAKE:

1 loaf (9"x 5") Aunt Snookum's Chocolate Pound Cake (page 115) or a store-bought pound cake loaf

3 tablespoons orange liqueur

1 pound ricotta cheese

2 tablespoons heavy cream or evaporated milk

¼ cup powdered sugar

2 tablespoons coarsely chopped unsalted almonds or pistachios

2 tablespoons coarsely chopped candied orange peel or citron

2 tablespoons miniature semisweet chocolate pieces

FROSTING:

⅓ cup shortening

3 to 4 tablespoons orange juice

2 teaspoons finely shredded orange peel

3 cups sifted powdered sugar

TO ASSEMBLE THE CAKE: Trim the crusts from the cake and cut the top off so the cake is flat. Cut the cake into 4 thin, even horizontal slices. Place each slice on a sheet of waxed paper; sprinkle 3 of the slices each with 1 tablespoon orange liqueur. Set aside.

In a blender or food processor, cream together the ricotta cheese, cream or milk, and powdered sugar until smooth. Scrape into a mixing bowl and stir in the nuts, orange peel or citron, and chocolate.

Place a large sheet of flexible freezer wrap on a baking sheet and put one of the 3 liqueur-soaked cake slices in the center of the wrap. Spread carefully with one-third of the cheese filling, to within ½ inch of the edges. Repeat with the remaining cake and filling, topping the stack with the cake slice not soaked with liqueur. Press the stack lightly to settle it.

FROSTING TIPS

- To frost cake layers, turn the bottom layer upside down, because the bottom of the cake is smoother and less likely to crumble or separate.
- Before frosting any cake, brush the crumbs off the surface to prevent them from getting mixed into the frosting.
- To prevent drips and drops of frosting from getting on the cake serving plate, first tear off several 2-inch wide strips of waxed paper. Slip the strips under all the edges of the cake; frost the cake as usual, then pull the waxed paper away and discard.

TO MAKE THE FROSTING: In a medium bowl, cream together the shortening and orange juice. Stir in the orange peel, then gradually stir in the powdered sugar and beat until smooth. The frosting will be somewhat stiff.

TO FREEZE: Cover the cake with freezer wrap and seal. Place in a box to protect it, if you like. Put the frosting in a rigid freezer container and cover. Label both and freeze for up to 2 months.

TO SERVE: Defrost frosting, covered, in the refrigerator for 4 hours. Unwrap the cake, place it on a serving platter, and defrost for 3 hours. (Do not defrost in a microwave oven.)

Stir the frosting until smooth. Spread a thin layer of frosting smoothly on the sides and top of the cake. If desired, put the remaining frosting in a pastry bag and decorate the cake. Refrigerate until serving time. Cut into 1-inch slices and serve on glass cake plates, if desired. Refrigerate leftovers, but do not refreeze.

Makes 1 cake (serves 8)

■ *Cassata a la Little Italy*

SILVER DECORATIVE BALLS

Although small silver decorative balls are a beautiful cake and cookie decoration, it is best not to eat them. Have your guests remove them, or remove them yourself, before eating.

Pies

PENNY'S NEVER-FAIL PIE CRUST

I made my first pie crust when I was in college. That crust was just as hard as the plate it sat on. So my roommate, Penny Satterwhite Collins, gave me this terrific recipe. If you overwork it, it may shrink when baked, but it stays flaky no matter what.

4 cups all-purpose flour
1 teaspoon salt
1$\frac{1}{3}$ cups shortening
1 egg
1 teaspoon white vinegar
$\frac{1}{2}$ cup milk

TO MAKE: In a large bowl, toss together the flour and salt. With a pastry blender or 2 knives, cut in the shortening until the mixture resembles coarse cornmeal. In a small bowl, mix together the egg, vinegar, and milk; stir into the flour mixture, mixing only until blended and the dough holds together in a ball. Cut the dough into 4 equal pieces.

TO MAKE SINGLE-CRUST PIES: With a floured rolling pin, using short, quick strokes, roll each portion out into a 12-inch circle on a lightly floured surface. Transfer to a 9-inch pie plate. Trim excess crust to a 1-inch overhang, turn under, and flute the edges.

TO MAKE DOUBLE-CRUST PIES: Roll out dough as for single-crust pies and fit 2 of the dough portions into pie plates. Trim the edge of the pastry even with the pie plate. Do not prick. Roll out the remaining 2 pieces to 10-inch circles and place on cardboard that is covered with plastic wrap.

TO FREEZE: *To freeze crusts in pie plates,* layer 2 sheets of plastic wrap between each crust and stack the crusts. To protect the edges of the crusts, invert a paper plate over the top crust and tape the edges of the plate to the pans. Wrap well in a large freezer bag or freezer wrap and seal. Label and freeze.

To freeze flat top crusts, cover each pie crust circle with 2 layers of plastic wrap and wrap well in a large freezer bag or freezer wrap and seal. Label and freeze for up to 2 months.

TO SERVE: *For single-crust (cream or chiffon) pies,* allow the crust to thaw completely. Prick crust with a fork. Line the shell with a double thickness of foil. Bake at 450°F for 8 minutes, remove foil, then continue baking for about 5 to 6 minutes, or until the crust is golden brown. Cool thoroughly before adding a cooked filling.

For pies baked with filling (single-crust chess, custard, pecan, or pumpkin pie), allow the shell to thaw slightly. Prepare the filling according to your favorite recipe. Pour the filling mixture into the unbaked pie shell and bake according to the recipe.

For double-crust (fruit or mincemeat) pie, allow the shell and a flat top crust to thaw completely. Prepare the filling according to your favorite recipe. Pour the filling into the pie shell and cover with the top crust. Trim excess top crust to a 1-inch overhang. Moisten the edges of the bottom crust, and fold the edges of the top crust under the bottom crust; then flute or crimp the edges. Cut slits in the top crust. Bake the pie according to the recipe instructions.

◆ *Makes 4 single-crust or 2 double-crust pie shells*

VARIATION: You can also make scrumptious cookies with this recipe: Roll it out to a 1/2-inch thickness, spread with butter, and sprinkle liberally with cinnamon and sugar. Cut into 1-inch squares or diamonds and bake at 425°F for 15 minutes, or until brown, fragrant, and baked through.

MEATLESS MINCEMEAT

Traditional mincemeats are made with lean beef and beef suet. Here's a recipe without the meat and fat, but with all the great spicy flavor of mincemeat. You don't want too much of the bitter white part of the citrus skins in the mix, so if the orange and lemon have a thick layer, cut some of it away and discard it before you process the fruits together.

1 large, thin-skinned orange, quartered and seeded
1 small lemon, quartered and seeded
3 pounds (about 9 medium) tart apples, quartered and cored
1 1/2 cups raisins
1 1/2 cups currants
1 1/2 cups apple cider or juice
3 cups firmly packed brown sugar
1 teaspoon ground cinnamon
1 teaspoon ground nutmeg
3/4 teaspoon ground cloves
1/2 teaspoon salt
1/4 cup brandy, rum, or bourbon

TO MAKE: In a food processor, chop the orange pieces, lemon pieces, and apples. Or, using a coarse blade, force the fruit through a food chopper or finely chop with a knife. Pour into a stainless steel or enameled kettle. Add the raisins, currants, and cider or juice and bring to a boil. Lower the heat and simmer, uncovered, for 15 minutes. Add the sugar, cinnamon, nutmeg, cloves, and salt. Simmer, uncovered, for 20 minutes longer, or until thick and most of the liquid has evaporated.

Cool the mixture quickly by placing the kettle in a sinkful of ice water. Stir in the brandy, rum, or bourbon.

TO FREEZE: Divide the mixture equally into 3 rigid freezer containers or freezer bags and seal. Label and freeze for up to 6 months.

TO SERVE: Each container has enough mincemeat for one 9-inch pie or six 4-inch tarts. Remove the amount you need from the freezer and defrost, covered, for 2 to 3 hours, or defrost in a microwave oven on 30 percent power for 4 to 5 minutes, stirring once.

Preheat the oven to 375°F. Pour the mincemeat into unbaked pie or tart shells and dot with butter (1 tablespoon total for 1 pie or 6 tarts). Cover with the top crust and cut slits in the crust, or make a lattice top crust with strips of dough. Sprinkle with sugar. Bake a 9-inch pie for 45 to 50 minutes and tarts for 35 to 40 minutes, or until golden. Cool thoroughly before serving.

Makes enough filling for three 9-inch pies or eighteen 4-inch tarts

■ *Meatless Mincemeat*

■ *Southern-Style Sweet Potato Custard*

SOUTHERN-STYLE SWEET POTATO CUSTARD

This custard makes a cozy dessert simply baked and served warm with lightly sweetened whipped cream; or you can bake it in a pie shell for a traditional holiday dessert. If the great taste of sweet potatoes isn't enough to win you over, consider the fact that they're virtually fat-free and loaded with vitamin C and beta-carotene.

1 cup whipping cream or evaporated milk
2 teaspoons vinegar
1 teaspoon baking soda
4 cups cooked, mashed sweet potatoes (fresh or canned)
1 cup sugar
2 teaspoons baking powder
1 teaspoon ground cinnamon
1 teaspoon ground ginger
1/2 teaspoon ground nutmeg
1/4 teaspoon salt
6 eggs

TO MAKE: In a small bowl, stir together the cream or milk, vinegar, and baking soda. In a large bowl, mix together the sweet potatoes, sugar, baking powder, cinnamon, ginger, nutmeg, salt, and eggs. Add the cream mixture and beat with an electric mixer set on high speed until smooth.

TO FREEZE: Line two 9-inch pie plates with plastic wrap. Divide the custard equally between the 2 pie plates.

Place in the freezer until the custard is frozen solid. Remove from the freezer and lift out the frozen custards with the plastic lining. If necessary, place a warm cloth on the bottom of the pie plate to help loosen the custard.

Wrap custard well in freezer wrap and seal. Label and return to the freezer for up to 6 weeks.

TO SERVE: Unwrap the custards. You may have to let the custard defrost partially to remove the last layer of plastic wrap.

To serve as custard dessert, put a frozen custard in a lightly greased pie plate and bake at 350°F for 60 to 65 minutes, or until a knife inserted in the center comes out clean. Serve warm or cold.

To serve as pie, put a frozen custard into an unbaked pastry-lined pie plate. Bake in a 350°F oven for 60 to 65 minutes, or until a knife inserted in the center comes out clean. Cool thoroughly before cutting. If desired, decorate with pastry cutouts.

Makes enough filling for two 9-inch custards or pies

PATTY'S SHOE

You may recognize this recipe as pâte à choux, which can be made into bite-size pastry cases (profiteroles) for pick-up desserts or made larger for cream puffs. Fill these pastries with whipped cream, ice cream, lemon curd, custard, or any flavor of mousse. Depending on the filling, top with hot fudge, toffee, or fruit sauce or simply dust with powdered sugar.

Remember that with the same recipe, you can make tiny hors d'oeuvres filled with minced crab or chicken salad or chunks of Brie or Saga cheese.

1 cup water
1/8 teaspoon salt
1/2 cup butter or margarine, softened
1 cup all-purpose flour
4 eggs, at room temperature

TO MAKE: Preheat the oven to 400°F.

In a medium saucepan, heat the water and salt to a boil. Add the butter; stir and heat until the butter is melted and the water is just returning to a boil. Add the flour all at once.

Reduce the heat to low and heat the mixture, stirring constantly, until it holds together in a mass. The texture will be smooth and will pull away from the pan easily. Remove the pan from the heat and let the mixture cool for 10 minutes.

Add the eggs, 1 at a time, and beat very well with a wooden spoon after each addition. Beat until the mixture is smooth and no longer slippery.

For small puffs (profiteroles), drop the batter onto a greased baking sheet by rounded teaspoonfuls, 2 inches apart. For cream puffs, drop by rounded tablespoonfuls, 3 inches apart. Bake profiteroles for about 20 minutes and cream puffs for 30 to 35 minutes, or until the puffs are golden and sound hollow when tapped.

Turn off the oven. Remove the puffs and make a tiny slit in the side near the bottom of each puff. Return to the oven with the door ajar about 5 minutes, to allow the steam to escape from the centers. Remove from the oven and cool thoroughly on wire racks.

TO FREEZE: Put the puffs on a baking sheet and place in the freezer for about 1 hour, until frozen solid. Wrap in freezer wrap, freezer bags, or rigid containers and seal. Label and return to the freezer for up to 3 months. Place in a box to protect them, if you like.

TO SERVE: Unwrap and defrost for 1 hour. To fill, either slice the tops off, fill with a spoon, and replace the tops or place the filling in a pastry bag and make a hole in the side of the puff with the pastry tip, then squeeze the filling into the center of the puff, repeating until all the puffs are filled.

Makes 4 dozen profiteroles or 1 dozen cream puffs

BUTTERCREAMS GALORE

Have at least a couple of flavored frostings in the freezer to top cupcakes, layer cakes, and cookies. Here's a reliable buttercream frosting and variations that freeze well. The basic recipe and all variations can be doubled.

⅓ **cup butter or margarine, softened, or shortening**
2 **teaspoons vanilla**
⅛ **teaspoon salt**
1 **pound sifted (about 4 cups) powdered sugar**
4 **to 6 tablespoons evaporated milk**

TO MAKE: In a large bowl, beat the butter, margarine or shortening, vanilla, and salt until fluffy. Gradually add the sugar, alternately with the milk. Continue beating until smooth and satiny.

TO FREEZE: Scrape the frosting into a rigid freezer container or freezer bag and seal. Label and freeze for up to 2 months. Frostings may soften slightly when defrosted.

TO SERVE: Defrost the frosting, covered, in the refrigerator overnight or at room temperature for 1 to 2 hours. Stir until smooth before using. If necessary, stir in additional powdered sugar.

Makes enough for a 2-layer 8-or 9-inch cake or 24 cupcakes

VARIATIONS: Chocolate Buttercream: Add ½ cup unsweetened cocoa powder with the butter, margarine, or shortening.

Cream Cheese Frosting: Substitute 6 ounces softened cream cheese for the butter, margarine, or shortening and reduce the milk to 2 to 3 teaspoons.

Mocha Buttercream: Add 2 teaspoons instant coffee crystals and ⅓ cup unsweetened cocoa powder with the butter, margarine, or shortening.

Orange or Lemon Buttercream: Substitute 4 tablespoons orange or lemon juice for the milk, omit the vanilla, and add ¼ teaspoon almond extract, if desired, and 2 to 3 teaspoons finely shredded orange or lemon peel.

Strawberry Buttercream: Substitute ⅓ cup pureed fresh or thawed frozen strawberries for the milk, omit the vanilla, and add 1 teaspoon lemon juice.

▪ *Patty's Shoe*

Cookies and Treats

THIS CHRISTMAS, WITH A FREEZER AND PANTRY FILLED WITH GOODIES, YOU'LL BE SO WELL PREPARED FOR THE HOLIDAY RUSH, YOU'LL GRACIOUSLY VOLUNTEER TO BRING YOUR HOMEMADE COOKIES AND CAKES TO NEIGHBORHOOD POTLUCK PARTIES OR THE OFFICE HOLIDAY BASH.

NATURALLY, YOU'LL WANT TO SAVE SOME COOKIES AND CANDIES

TO SHARE WITH FAMILY AND FRIENDS ON ALL THE SPECIAL DAYS AND EVENINGS OF THE SEASON. CHILDREN WILL BE DAZZLED BY FANCIFULLY DECORATED GINGERBREAD PEOPLE ON THEIR PLATES OR HUNG FROM A WREATH OR CHRISTMAS TREE. AND ADULTS WILL BE IMPRESSED WITH RUM BALLS AND DELICATELY TEXTURED BUTTERY SPRITZ COOKIES.

MEXICAN CHOCOLATE SUGAR COOKIES

Crisp and sugary on the outside, these rich chocolate cookies have a hint of cinnamon and a chewy inside texture. These cookies are strong and mail well.

¾ cup shortening
1 cup sugar
1 egg
¼ cup light corn syrup
2 ounces unsweetened chocolate, melted
1¾ cups all-purpose flour
2 teaspoons baking soda
1 teaspoon ground cinnamon
¼ teaspoon salt
1 cup semisweet chocolate pieces
¼ cup sugar, for coating

TO MAKE: In a large bowl, cream together the shortening, 1 cup sugar, and egg with an electric mixer. Stir in the corn syrup and unsweetened chocolate.

In a small bowl, stir together the flour, baking soda, cinnamon, and salt. Stir into the shortening mixture to make a stiff dough. Add the chocolate pieces.

Pour ¼ cup sugar into another small bowl or onto a saucer. Shape the dough into 1-inch balls and roll each in sugar.

TO FREEZE: Line a baking sheet with plastic wrap or waxed paper and add the cookie dough balls, placing them close together. Place in the freezer for about 2 hours, until frozen solid. Put frozen cookie balls in freezer bags or rigid containers and seal. Label and return to the freezer. Freeze dough or baked cookies for up to 6 months.

TO SERVE: Remove the amount of cookies you want to bake from the freezer and place them on an ungreased baking sheet, about 3 inches apart. Let thaw at room temperature for 30 minutes. Meanwhile, preheat the oven to 350°F. Bake thawed cookies for about 10 minutes, or until puffed and the tops crack. Let stand a few minutes before removing from the pan. Cool on a wire rack.

Makes 4 dozen cookies

COOKIE-MAKING TIPS

- Form dough for rolled or drop cookies in 2-inch-diameter rolls. Wrap and refrigerate until chilled. Then, cut off 1-inch-thick slices; cut the slices into quarters and drop into freezer bags or rigid containers. Label, seal, and freeze. To bake, place frozen quarters on baking sheets. It may be necessary to bake about 1 minute more than the recipe calls for.
- For jumbo-size drop cookies of uniform size, form them with a small ice cream scoop with a spring-action release.
- It takes almost the same amount of time to make double or triple the amount of cookie dough as it does to make the single recipe. Go ahead and make extra dough while you're at it, then freeze the extra to bake when you're in a hurry.

■ *Mexican Chocolate Sugar Cookies*

BUTTERY SPRITZ COOKIES

Christmas classics, spritz cookies can be made in many shapes and flavors. Shape them with a cookie press or cookie "gun" or put the dough in a pastry bag and force through a wide pastry tip. Decorate with colored sprinkles, candied cherries, or a dusting of sugar.

1 cup butter
2/3 cup sugar
2 egg yolks
1 teaspoon vanilla
2 cups all-purpose flour
Colored sprinkles or sugar (optional)
Candied cherries, halved or cut up
    (optional)

TO MAKE: Preheat the oven to 375°F.

In a large bowl, cream the butter until light and fluffy. Add the sugar gradually and continue beating until fluffy. Add the egg yolks and vanilla; beat well. Mix in the flour by hand just until blended; do not overmix.

Spoon the mixture into a cookie press, cookie "gun," or pastry bag fitted with a wide star tip or a plain tube to form wreaths, canes, or pretzels. Or, using a cookie press, press cookies in star, tree, wreath, or bar shapes onto ungreased baking sheets. Decorate with colored sprinkles or sugar or press candied cherries, if using, into cookies.

Bake for 8 to 10 minutes, or just until firm, not brown. Remove to wire racks to cool completely.

TO FREEZE: Wrap the cookies well in freezer wrap or freezer bags and seal; because cookies are very fragile, place in boxes or plastic containers to protect. Label and freeze for up to 6 months.

TO SERVE: Defrost, still wrapped, at room temperature for 20 minutes.

Makes 3½ to 5 dozen, depending on size

VARIATIONS: Almond Spritz: Add ½ teaspoon almond extract with the vanilla. Sprinkle with ½ cup very finely chopped (not ground) toasted almonds before baking.

Orange Spritz: Add 2 teaspoons finely shredded orange peel with the vanilla.

Chocolate Dips: Form and bake any flavor spritz cookies in bar or log shapes (if making almond spritz cookies, omit the almonds). To serve, chop ⅓ cup toasted pecans or almonds and set aside. Melt together in a small heavy saucepan ½ cup semisweet chocolate pieces and 1 teaspoon shortening over very low heat. Dip one end of each cookie in the melted chocolate, then roll in the chopped nuts. Let set on waxed paper until the chocolate has cooled and set.

PECAN CRESCENTS

A tender butter cookie, these simply melt in your mouth. They're a traditional Christmas "must" for many families.

1 cup butter, softened
¼ cup powdered sugar
1 tablespoon water
1 teaspoon vanilla
2 cups all-purpose flour
2 cups very finely chopped pecans
Powdered sugar, for coating

TO MAKE: Preheat the oven to 325°F. In a large bowl, cream the butter until fluffy and white. Gradually add ¼ cup sugar, then beat in the water and vanilla until fluffy. By hand, stir in the flour and pecans. Cover and chill for at least 1 hour. (The dough will be a little sticky.)

Using about 1 tablespoon of dough each, form the dough into small logs, each about 3 inches long. Bend each log into a crescent shape. Place on a baking sheet and bake for 20 minutes, or until very lightly browned. Let cool on the baking sheet for 5 minutes.

Put some powdered sugar in a small bowl and roll the hot cookies in it. You can hold the cookies with 2 forks, if you like. The sugar will melt onto the cookies. Place on a wire rack to cool completely.

TO FREEZE: Wrap the cookies well in freezer wrap or freezer bags and seal; because cookies are very fragile, place in boxes or plastic containers to protect. Label and freeze for up to 6 months.

TO SERVE: Defrost, still wrapped, at room temperature for 20 minutes. Roll cookies again in powdered sugar, if desired.

Makes 4 dozen cookies

VARIATION: To make smaller cookies, use about 1 teaspoon of dough to make 1-inch crescents. Bake for 15 minutes. Makes about 12 dozen.

▪ *Buttery Spritz Cookies (left)*

131

PUMPKIN DROP COOKIES

Even your favorite "cookie monster" will love these nutritious cookies.

1/2 cup butter or margarine
1 cup sugar
1 egg
1 cup canned pumpkin
1 teaspoon vanilla
2 cups all-purpose flour
1 teaspoon baking soda
3/4 teaspoon ground cinnamon
1/4 teaspoon salt
1/4 teaspoon ground nutmeg
1 cup raisins
1 cup chopped pecans or walnuts

TO MAKE: Preheat the oven to 375°F. Grease the baking sheets.

In a large bowl, cream together the butter or margarine and sugar until light and fluffy. Add the egg, pumpkin, and vanilla; mix well.

In a medium bowl, stir together the flour, baking soda, cinnamon, salt, and nutmeg. Add gradually to the pumpkin mixture and stir until blended. Stir in the raisins and nuts.

Drop the dough by rounded teaspoons onto the baking sheets. Bake for 12 to 15 minutes, or until lightly browned. Transfer to wire racks to cool completely.

TO FREEZE: Line a flat, shallow, rigid plastic container with waxed paper. Put 1 layer of cookies on the waxed paper, then cover with another layer of waxed paper and continue layering until the container is full. Cover with a tight-fitting lid. Label and freeze for up to 6 months.

TO SERVE: Defrost cookies, still wrapped, for 30 minutes. Meanwhile, make the icing.

In a small bowl, mix together 2 cups powdered sugar, 2 tablespoons butter or margarine, 2 teaspoons finely shredded orange peel, and 2 tablespoons orange juice. Spread on cookies. Garnish with orange peel.

Makes 4 dozen cookies

- *Pecan Crescents (left); Pumpkin Drop Cookies (below)*

HONEY CAKES

German bakers start their holiday cookie-making in November by baking these traditional spicy cookies, which get chewier and softer as they age at room temperature for several weeks. These are good candidates for mailing.

CAKES:

3 cups all-purpose flour

1¼ teaspoons ground nutmeg

1¼ teaspoons ground cinnamon

½ teaspoon baking soda

½ teaspoon ground cloves

½ teaspoon ground allspice

1 egg

¾ cup firmly packed dark brown sugar

½ cup honey

½ cup dark molasses

½ cup chopped almonds

½ cup chopped mixed candied fruits and peels

1 cup slivered blanched almonds

Red and green maraschino cherries

GLAZE:

1 cup powdered sugar

¼ cup light rum

1 tablespoon water

TO MAKE THE CAKES: In a medium bowl, stir together the flour, nutmeg, cinnamon, baking soda, cloves, and allspice. Set aside.

In a large bowl, beat the egg; add the sugar and beat until well combined. Stir in the honey and molasses. Add the dry ingredients, beating until well combined. Stir in the chopped nuts and fruits and peels. Chill for several hours or overnight.

Preheat the oven to 350°F. On a floured surface, roll half of the dough into a rectangle ¼-inch thick. Trim the uneven edges. Cut the

dough into 1" x 1½" rectangles. Press two slivers of almond into the top of each cookie, and garnish each with one-half of a red and/or a green cherry. Bake the cookies on a greased baking sheet for 10 to 12 minutes, or until lightly browned.

TO MAKE THE GLAZE: While the cookies are baking, combine all ingredients in a small bowl. Stir until smooth. Place wire racks over sheets of waxed paper to catch drips of glaze. Remove the cookies to the racks and brush the tops with the glaze while the cookies are still hot. Let cool completely.

TO STORE: Place in airtight containers or cookie tins. If the cookies get hard during storage, place a slice of raw apple in the container for 1 day, then discard the apple. Store at room temperature for at least 2 weeks and up to 1 month.

TO FREEZE: Place aged cookies in airtight containers. Label and freeze for up to 6 months.

TO SERVE: Defrost at room temperature for 30 minutes.

Makes 12 to 13 dozen cookies

For loved ones who are away during the holidays, a box of your homemade cookies and candies is one of the warmest ways to send your love. See page 140 for special instructions for mailing food.

■ *Honey Cakes (left)*

GINGERBREAD PEOPLE

Gather some children to help make and decorate these fun cookies. Get out your garlic press and force the cookie dough through it to make "hair" for the people. If you plan to hang the cookies, punch a hole in the tops before baking.

½ cup butter or margarine, softened

1 cup firmly packed light brown sugar

1½ cups light molasses

⅔ cup water

6½ cups all-purpose flour

2 teaspoons baking soda

2 teaspoons salt

2 teaspoons ground ginger

1 teaspoon ground cinnamon

1 teaspoon ground allspice

½ teaspoon ground cloves

Raisins, semisweet chocolate pieces, colored sprinkles, sugar, and/or nuts

TO MAKE: In a large bowl, beat the butter or margarine and sugar until creamy. Add the molasses and beat until blended, then mix in the water. In another large bowl, stir together the flour, baking soda, salt, ginger, cinnamon, allspice, and cloves. Gradually beat into the butter mixture until the dough is stiff and blended together. (Stir in the last of the flour with a spoon until well mixed.) Divide the dough into quarters. Cover and refrigerate for at least 4 hours.

TO BAKE: Preheat the oven to 350°F. Lightly grease baking sheets.

Roll the dough with a rolling pin to ¼-inch thickness. Cut out cookies with people-shaped cookie cutters. Transfer to a baking sheet. If you're adding "hair," dampen the

head of the "person" with water, then force a bit of dough through a garlic press and arrange hair on the head. If you're adding eyes or buttons, use the raisins, chocolate pieces, sprinkles, sugar, and/or nuts, and press them into the dough before baking. If you use silver decorative balls, remember to remove them before eating.

Bake 10 to 12 minutes, or until lightly browned. Remove to wire racks and cool completely.

To freeze: Line a flat, shallow, rigid plastic container with waxed paper. Put 1 layer of cookies on the waxed paper, then cover with another layer of waxed paper and continue layering until the container is full. Cover with a tight-fitting lid. Label and freeze for up to 6 months.

To serve: Defrost, still wrapped, at room temperature for 30 minutes. If desired, spread the cookies with icing or put icing in a decorating tube to make faces, clothes, or shoes on the gingerbread people.

To make decorating icing, combine 2 cups sifted powdered sugar and enough milk or light cream (2 to 3 tablespoons) to make it a piping consistency. Tint with 2 or 3 drops of food coloring, if desired.

To make royal icing, mix 2 tablespoons meringue powder with ¼ cup water; beat to stiff peaks. Add 2 cups sifted powdered sugar and beat to desired consistency.

Makes 4 dozen cookies

▪ *Gingerbread People*

RUM BALLS

To serve at a party, stack these potent little candies in a pyramid on a serving plate, then dust with powdered sugar for a snowlike effect. Or, roll each ball in powdered sugar and place in a fluted paper candy cup. Box them and mail them off to a long-distance friend.

3 cups crushed vanilla wafers
1 cup sifted powdered sugar
1½ cups finely chopped pecans
2 tablespoons unsweetened cocoa powder
2 tablespoons light corn syrup
½ cup rum

TO MAKE: In a large bowl, mix together the cookie crumbs, powdered sugar, pecans, and cocoa powder. Add the corn syrup and rum; blend well with a wooden spoon until evenly moist. Using about 2 teaspoons for each, shape into 1-inch balls.

TO FREEZE: Place the candies on a waxed paper-lined baking sheet. Freeze for about 1 hour, or until firm. Put the candy in freezer bags or rigid containers and seal. Label and freeze for up to 3 months.

TO SERVE: Unwrap and defrost at room temperature for about 15 minutes. Roll in powdered sugar, if you like.

Makes about 5 dozen

VARIATION: Substitute orange juice for the rum.

▪ *Rum Balls*

POLLY POTTER'S SUGARED WALNUTS

Sometime in the late 1970s, Polly Potter called a radio talkshow in Salt Lake City and shared this recipe…and I've made these tasty nuts many times since. Leave some in a candy dish at a party and they'll disappear in a flash. Or, fill pretty jars and give them as gifts. (Thank you, Polly, wherever you are.)

1½ cups firmly packed light brown sugar
½ cup butter
¼ cup water
1½ pounds walnuts

TO MAKE: Heat a large skillet over medium-low heat. Add the sugar, butter, and water to the skillet and stir until the butter is melted and the mixture bubbles. Carefully add the nuts and stir constantly for 12 to 15 minutes, or until the sugar mixture thickens and nuts have a slightly sugary look. Turn the nuts out onto a large heat-proof platter to cool thoroughly. Break into bite-size pieces.

TO FREEZE: Transfer cooled nuts to freezer bags or rigid containers and seal. Label and freeze for up to 3 months.

TO SERVE: Defrost at room temperature for 30 minutes.

Makes 2¼ pounds

TIPS FOR WRAPPING AND MAILING COOKIES

- Choose cookies that are strong enough to arrive whole and that will stay fresh during their trip. The best cookies for mailing are those that are firm, but not brittle; crisp, but not delicate; or soft and flexible.
- Glazed cookies travel well, but don't send cookies with soft frostings.
- Wrap cookies individually or back-to-back in plastic wrap or foil, then pack in tins or a rigid plastic container.
- Pack soft and crisp cookies separately to preserve their textures.
- Put the cookie container in a cardboard box and cushion the container with popped popcorn (air-popped is best, but any kind will do) or crumpled newspaper.
- Mark the box "fragile" and tape it securely with packaging (not masking) tape.
- Send the box first class or priority mail to ensure that it arrives while the cookies are still fresh.

■ *Polly Potter's Sugared Walnuts (left); Fruit-Granola Rolls (right)*

◆ FRUIT-GRANOLA ROLLS

1 package (12 ounces) pitted prunes
1 cup granola, crushed
1 cup golden raisins
1/2 cup dried figs
1/2 cup dried apricots
1/2 cup walnuts (toasted, if desired)
1/4 teaspoon ground cinnamon
Crushed granola, for coating

TO MAKE: In a large bowl, combine the prunes, granola, raisins, figs, apricots, walnuts, and cinnamon. Put about a third of the mixture in the bowl of a food processor and process until it is blended and forms a ball. Repeat with the remaining fruit mixture. Or, force the ingredients through the fine blade of a food grinder.

Divide the mixture in half and place on sheets of waxed paper. Form each half into a log about 11 inches long. Sprinkle a board with crushed granola; roll logs to coat. Wrap well.

TO FREEZE: Place wrapped logs in freezer bags or plastic wrap and foil and seal. Label and freeze for up to 2 months.

TO SERVE: Unwrap and defrost at room temperature for 30 minutes. Roll in additional crushed granola, if desired. Cut into 1/4-inch thick slices.

Makes two 11-inch logs

SOURCES

Most of the supplies called for in the directions for the projects in this book are available in craft stores. If you have difficulty finding specific items, contact the manufacturer for a listing of suppliers in your area.

ACCENT PAINTS
300 East Main Street
Lake Zurich, IL 60047
(708) 540-1604

COATS & CLARK/ANCHOR (EMBROIDERY FLOSS)
Consumer Service Dept.
30 Patewood Drive
Greenville, SC 29615
(800) 648-1479

DEKA SILK SALTS
P.O. Box 309
Morrisville, VT 05661
(802) 888-4217

DELTA PAINTS
2550 Pellissier Place
Whittier, CA 90601
(800) 423-4135

FREUDENBERG NONWOVENS (PELLON)
20 Industrial Avenue
Chelmsford, MA 01824
(508) 454-0461

C.M. OFFRAY AND SON (RIBBONS)
Route 24
Chester, NJ 07930
(908) 879-4700

V.I.P. FABRICS
1412 Broadway
New York, NY 10018
(800) 847-4064

WALNUT HOLLOW WOODCRAFT STORE
Hwy. 23 North
Dodgeville, WI 53533
(800) 950-5101

ZWEIGART (NEEDLEWORK FABRICS)
Weston Canal Plaza
2 Riverview Drive
Somerset, NJ 08873
(908) 271-1949

DESIGNERS

Our special thanks to the following designers who contributed projects for this book:

YVONNE BEECHER—Sampler Ornaments, page 31; Father Christmas, page 36; Clay Bead Jewelry, page 51; Patchwork Vest, page 58

KOLLATH/McCANN—Holiday Pots, page 18

JOSEPH RICHINELLI—Sleigh Full of Flowers, page 20

GINGER HANSEN SHAFER—Welcome Mat, page 16; Wooden Angels, page 34; Rainbow Scarves and Neckties, page 44; Glorious Gifts, page 55; Beautiful Boxes, page 61

MIMI SHIMMIN—Appliqué House Place Mats, page 22; Lace Ornaments, page 28; Bow-and-Star Pullover, page 58

JACKIE SMYTH—Counting-the-Days Advent Calendar, page 41

PROP CREDITS

WE ARE GRATEFUL TO THE GARDEN SHOP IN GLEN RIDGE, NEW JERSEY, FOR THE LOAN OF THE FOLLOWING FINE ITEMS FOR USE IN THE PHOTOGRAPHY. THOSE ITEMS NOT INDIVIDUALLY LISTED WE OBTAINED PRIVATELY.

CRAFT PROPS:

Page 19: topiaries; **Page 67**: ornaments.

WE ARE GRATEFUL TO PIER ONE IMPORTS IN NEW YORK, NEW YORK, FOR THE LOAN OF THE FOLLOWING FINE ITEMS FOR USE IN THE PHOTOGRAPHY. THOSE ITEMS NOT INDIVIDUALLY LISTED WE OBTAINED PRIVATELY.

FOOD PROPS:

Page 75: stemware; **Page 79**: plate, salt & pepper; **Page 82**: plate & fork; **Page 84**: platter, candlesticks, glasses; **Page 87**: all dinnerware, baskets, fish, brush; **Page 97**: marble board & wine glass; **Page 118**: espresso set, candlesticks; **Page 130**: plaid dessert plates & demitasse set; **Page 132**: red plate, candlestick; **Page 134**: tins; **Page 138**: wooden box; **Page 139**: green wooden platter.